Chuckle Chants

Choral and Shared Reading Activities

by Kathryn A. Gangel

illustrated by Chris Nye

With love to God, my family—David, Marshall, Hollyann, Mark, Kaitlyn, and Gavin, plus friends and students at Springfield.

Editorial Director: Kristin Eclov

Editor: Cindy Barden

Cover and Interior Design: Good Neighbor Press, Inc.

Fearon Teacher Aids products were formerly manufactured and distributed by American Teaching Aids, Inc., a subsidiary of Silver Burdett Ginn, and are now manufactured and distributed by Frank Schaffer Publications, Inc. FEARON, FEARON TEACHER AIDS, and the FEARON balloon logo are marks used under license from Simon & Schuster, Inc.

Fearon Teacher Aids
A Division of Frank Schaffer Publications, Inc.
23740 Hawthorne Boulevard
Torrance, CA 90505

Table of Contents

FE11004 © 1999 Fearon Teacher Aids

Table of Contents

Table of Contents

FE11004 © 1999 Fearon Teacher Aids

Table of Contents

FE11004 © 1999 Fearon Teacher Aids

The Importance of Rhythm and Rhyme

Can you recall the words from popular songs you heard long ago, yet sometimes forget a phone number you just dialed? Can you recite all the words to an advertisement jingle that hasn't played for ten years, yet fail to remember a friend's address? It appears that our minds can replay these tunes from our past with only a slight conscious effort.

Commercials employ jingles and songs that contain rhythm and rhyme. Advertisement producers have used the appeal of rhythm and rhyme to successfully promote their products. Because of subconscious attraction to rhythm and rhyme, we can easily recall commercial jingles and songs from our childhood.

Students are especially drawn to verses with rhythm and rhyme. They repeat jump-rope chants, television jingles, nursery rhymes, and whimsical songs. They particularly enjoy those with an element of silliness or humor. As teachers and parents, we should use this natural attraction to rhythm and rhyme to facilitate learning and memorization. Chanting verses, songs, or poems is an entertaining way to learn. Rhythm, rhyme, and repetition can be a means for recalling and retaining information and introducing new content.

FE11004 © 1999 Fearon Teacher Aids

About Chuckle Chants

Chuckle Chants is a collection of chants created for choral reading in the classroom. These chants were written for students to read orally in unison, but are suitable for individual recitation and can be read silently for enjoyment and reinforcement of reading skills. The chants contain rhythm, rhyme, and repetition, which make it easy for students to participate.

Accompanying each chant is a page of suggestions for related activities to enhance the topic of the chant and extend learning. While the chants reinforce vocabulary, comprehension, reading, and speaking skills, the accompanying activities lead to further exploration of topics. By relating the topics of chants to other subjects, their content can be extended to other areas in the curriculum.

The activities include suggestions for creative writing, language arts, science, social studies, math, and art activities. A short bibliography is included on many activity pages, and related topics are included for all chants.

The puzzle pages reinforce content, spelling, vocabulary, following directions, identifying rhyming words, finding antonyms, alphabetizing, and classifying. Students can solve the puzzles independently or work with a partner. An answer key is provided for each puzzle page.

I hope you and your students will enjoy the chants and activities and share a few chuckles along the way.

Kathryn A. Gangel

FE11004 © 1999 Fearon Teacher Aids

How to Incorporate Choral Reading in the Classroom

In choral reading there are numerous ways to recite a verse or chant. This book provides two scripted options for each chant. However, you can vary the options by incorporating the different approaches described below. When presenting choral reading, choose an approach that best suits the needs and ability levels of your students. Experiment with the different scripted options and approaches to add variety to the choral reading experience.

When using the suggested options, assign groups or individuals to each of the numbers within the options. The parts can be assigned by reading ability or randomly by seating positions in the classroom. Please note, the scripted options are only suggestions and can be transferred from one chant to another at your discretion.

In choral reading there are several basic approaches for reciting a selection. One simple method is the repetitive approach. In this method the teacher recites one line at a time. The students immediately repeat the line after the teacher, using the same rhythm and pitch. This approach is appropriate to use for first-time exposure to choral reading.

Another choral reading method is the refrain approach. The teacher or student leader begins reading the verses and the class recites the chorus or refrain. After completing the chant successfully in this manner, the class can be divided into groups. Students with higher reading abilities can read the verse and the remaining students can recite the refrain.

Another approach to choral reading incorporates solo voices. After being introduced to the chant, volunteers are assigned lines, phrases, or verses to read by themselves. The solo voice approach can be used in combination with the refrain approach.

A fourth method to employ for the enjoyment of choral reading is an antiphonal or dialogue approach. This method employs two groups of students reading alternate lines. This approach works well with chants that have some dialogue or lines that require emphasis. Reading these lines alternately shows contrast.

The most commonly used, yet the most difficult type of choral reading approach, is reading in unison. This method can be complex because it requires all students to read entire selections together. While engaged in the enjoyment of participation, the students must coordinate the tempo, rhythm, and pitch simultaneously.

Remember, there is no one prescribed way to enjoy choral reading. Explore the different options and approaches for each chant to discover what matches and reinforces your students' abilities and interests.

FE11004 © 1999 Fearon Teacher Aids

Getting Started with Choral Readings

To begin the experience of choral reading in your classroom, choose a chant you feel your students will particularly enjoy. It could be one related to the content of a lesson or one with a humorous appeal that you use for comic relief in addition to reinforcing skills. After making your choice, read the selection carefully, noting how you want students to interpret the lines and verses. Reread the chant several times orally. Then plan how to introduce the elements listed below. Mark the text for easy recall of your decisions.

Decide on the tempo or speed which you and your class will read each line. Become familiar with the rhythm and determine which words to stress to give the chant a predictable beat. Students will need to practice the rhythm, so select the words or phrases to be emphasized.

Decide on the pitch of students' voices. Choose which lines students should read in a soft or loud tone.

Review the punctuation. It is important for students to know where to pause or stop when reading.

Conduct a short discussion about the topic or content of the selection. Have students listen to the chant as you read it. This gives them an opportunity to hear the established rhythm, rhyme scheme, and tempo.

Show students the text by distributing copies or displaying the chant on a chart or overhead projector. Reread the chant and discuss the content, the characters and plot, and definitions of any unfamiliar words.

Avoid in-depth analysis of each line so the mood of the chant remains. Again model the chant, this time emphasizing each line while students silently read along.

To help students begin to read and speak in unison, read one verse or section at a time and encourage them to join in. Continue to read the chant slowly, having students repeat the verses until they can recite the entire chant if using the unison approach.

There are no specifications on the number of times to practice. Stop the activity before the students become weary or lose interest.

Finally, add special touches to your choral reading performance by adding effects or actions. Physical actions, like clapping and body movements, help students comprehend the meaning and the mood. Remember to invite students to contribute their ideas and suggestions on how to say or act out the lines. Their interpretations will add to the excitement of the activity and will encourage them to be creative and use their imaginations. Choral reading involves active participation. Students' contributions will give them ownership of the activity, providing an enjoyable and exciting opportunity for learning.

FE11004 © 1999 Fearon Teacher Aids

Benefits of Choral Reading

Choral reading is for everyone.

- It provides opportunities for students to read passages together, allowing those with stronger reading abilities to begin the activity as leaders, while inviting shy students and those with weaker reading skills to read without fear of error.
- Students model after the more advanced readers as the reading passage is repeated.
- Those with speech difficulties can hear and copy correct speech patterns in a stress-free experience.
- In addition to boosting students' self-confidence, choral reading offers flexibility in meeting individual needs.
- Some students can be assigned an easier refrain or phrase, while others read the verse.
- Choral reading draws on different strengths and provides opportunities for everyone to shine.
- Participating in choral reading can promote the acquisition of language skills and increase student's self-esteem as they actively participate in a rewarding activity.

Choral reading provides opportunities for teamwork.

- A successful choral reading experience often involves groups of students planning the presentation of a chant.
- As a team, students work together to plan the tempo, interpretation, hand movements, pitch of voice, etc., to deliver the best recitation.

Choral reading promotes the acquisition of language through the development of fluency in reading and speaking.

- Word recognition, vocabulary development, comprehension, intonation, reading rate, and speaking skills can be improved.
- Repeated reading increases decoding rate and accuracy.

- As students become familiar with the words, they can focus on content rather than decoding.
- Since students are attracted to rhythm and rhyme, choral reading provides an easy and appealing way to develop and strengthen these components of reading.

Choral reading promotes the ability to follow directions and helps students sharpen listening skills.

- When learning to recite a chant, students must listen carefully to read, repeat, and imitate with the same intensity modeled by the teacher.
- The process also requires students to follow directions to read assigned parts and perform movements when appropriate.

Choral reading can be a springboard for developing students' creativity and enjoyment of poetry.

- The enjoyment students receive from reading aloud may encourage them to write their own poetry.
- As they participate in choral reading, students gain an appreciation for poetry through exposure to different elements of writing style.

Choral reading can extend learning across the curriculum by providing information about different subjects.

- The subject content can encourage students to satisfy their curiosity by investigating the topic and doing additional reading.

Best of all, choral reading helps build a rapport between the teacher and students. Students have a good time because their teacher is having fun!

References

Anthony, R. M. "Success with Choral Speaking." *Learning* 94 22 (1994): 66–67.

Danielson, K. E., and S. C. Dauer. "Celebrate Poetry Through Creative Drama." *Reading Horizons* 31 (1990): 138–148.

Gallagher, J. "Giving Voice to Poetry." *Ohio Reading Teacher* 29 (1994): 7–9.

Gangel, K. A. *Confetti: A Crazy, Corny Collection of Choral Reading Activities for the Classroom.* Wright Group Publishing, Inc. 1995.

Guthrie, B. "Effective Strategies for Teaching Fluency." *Ohio Reading Teacher* 25 (1991): 39–41.

Kormanski, L. M. "Using Poetry in the Intermediate Grades." *Reading Horizons* 32 (1992): 184–190.

Leidholdt, L. M. "They Can All Sound Good." *Reading Horizons* 29 (1989): 117–122.

McCauley, J. K., and D. S. McCauley. "Using Choral Reading to Promote Language Learning for ESL Students." *The Reading Teacher* 45 (1992): 526–533.

Miccinati, J. L. "Using Prosodic Cues to Teach Oral Reading Fluency." *The Reading Teacher* 39 (1985): 206–212.

Pennock, C. "Choral Reading of Poetry Improves Reading Fluency." *Highway One* 7 (1984): 21–22.

Stewig, J. W. "Choral Speaking: Who Has the Time? Why Take the Time?" *Childhood Education* 58 (1981): 25–29.

Swanson, B. B. "Reading Fluency and the Novice Reader." *Reading Horizons* 30 (1990): 265–270.

Cupcake Critters

Options

A	B	
1	1	We found a box of cupcakes In the park, all a-glitter.
2		So we took the box home To our new baby-sitter.
All	All	The box began to shiver. The box began to shake. The lid popped open. Out hopped a cupcake.
1	2	It hopped across the floor Like a small, wild critter.
2		'Til it was put back in the box By our new baby-sitter.
All	All	The box began to shiver. The box began to shake. The lid popped open. Out hopped a cupcake.

FE11004 © 1999 Fearon Teacher Aids

Cupcake Critters *(cont'd)*

1	2	It hopped across the floor.
		It was not a quitter.
2		Then we put it in the box,
		That wild, cupcake critter.

All	All	The box began to shiver.
		The box began to shake.
		The lid popped open.
		Out hopped a cupcake.

1	2	It hopped across the floor
		To our new baby-sitter.
2		It said, "Hello there,"
		And then the critter bit her.

All	All	The box began to shiver.
		The box began to shake.
		The lid popped open.
		Out hopped 40 cupcakes.

1	2	Now they all live in our house,
		Those wild cupcake critters.
		And no one wants to be
		Our new baby-sitter.

FE11004 © 1999 Fearon Teacher Aids

Cupcake Critter Puzzle

Circle all words in the poem that contain the letter *i*. If the sound is a long *i*, put a macron (⁻) over the *i*. Capture the cupcake critters by writing words from the poem that contain the letter *i* in the puzzle spaces.

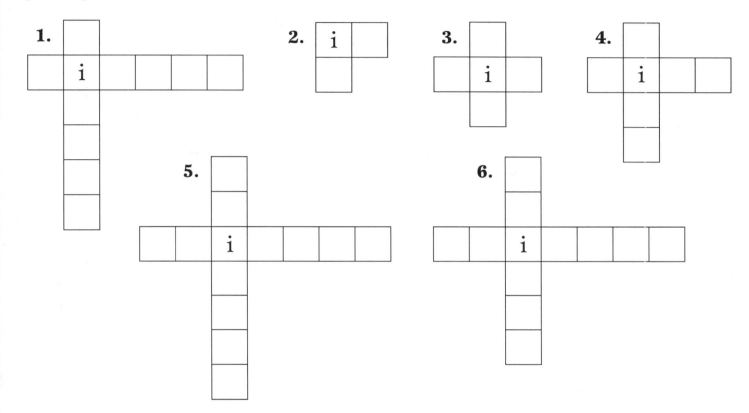

1.

2. i

3. i

4. i

5. i

6. i

◆ **Bonus:** Unscramble the letters to answer the riddle.

Question: Who makes clothes for cupcake critters' babies?

Answer:

A _ i _ _ _ _

_ _ _ i _ _ _ _ _

FE11004 © 1999 Fearon Teacher Aids

Cupcake Critter Words

How many words can you find in *cupcake critter*? You should be able to find at least 30. Write your words in the cupcake below.

Words must be three or more letters long. If a letter appears only once in *cupcake critter*, you can only use it once in a word (like the letter *k*). Here are the letters you can use:

a c c c e e i k p r r t t u

FE11004 © 1999 Fearon Teacher Aids

Cupcake Critter Activities

Color the Critters

Make a copy of the poem for each student. Have students color the Cupcake Critters with crayons or markers.

Compare and Contrast

Read the story about the Gingerbread Man to the class. Ask students how the Gingerbread Man is like the Cupcake Critters. How is he different?

Rhyme Time

Have students brainstorm a list of words or two-word phrases that rhyme with *critter*. Make another list of words or two-word phrases that rhyme with *cupcake*.

What Happened Next?

Students can write a sequel to the story about the Cupcake Critter. What did the Cupcake Critter and its friends do next? Tell about other problems they may have caused.

Draw an Ending

Students can draw pictures showing what could have happened next in the poem. Have them add captions under the pictures to explain what is happening.

Edible Cupcake Critters

Students can create their own edible Cupcake Critters. Spread soft or whipped frosting on top of a cupcake. Students can use their imaginations and several types of candy (gumdrops, sprinkles, jelly beans, shoe-string licorice) to decorate cupcakes to look like Cupcake Critters. Construction-paper legs and arms can be taped to the outside of the cupcake wrappers.

A Story Box

Students can make story boxes by covering small boxes with construction paper. On the top of the box, write the title of the poem. Have them draw a picture on each side of the box showing the major events that happened in the poem. Display story boxes.

Related Topics

cupcakes, snacks, nutrition, pests, baby-sitters, boxes, litter, recycling

Hey Spooky Spider!

Options

A	B	
1	1	Hey spooky spider, You're getting close to me.
1	2	I will not mess with you, If you just let me be.
All	All	Hey spooky spider, What are you going to do? If you don't bother me, I won't bother you!
1	1	Hey spooky spider, You're crawling up my arm.
3	4	Please just go away, I will not do you harm.
All	All	Hey spooky spider, What are you going to do? If you don't bother me, I won't bother you!
1	1	Hey spooky spider, You're crawling under my chair.
5	6	Oh, spooky spider, I cannot find you there.
All	All	Hey spooky spider, What are you going to do? If you don't bother me, I won't bother you!
1	1	Hey spooky spider, Don't give me a fright.
7	8	I am kind of worried. I may not sleep tonight!
All	All	Hey spooky spider, What are you going to do? If you don't bother me, I won't bother you!

FE11004 © 1999 Fearon Teacher Aids

Hey Spooky Spider! Puzzle

Fill in the word web by writing words from the poem that have a similar meaning to the words below.

across
2. scare
7. creeping
8. to bother
12. frightening

down
1. fretted
3. this evening
4. hurt
5. myself
6. limb
7. near
9. slumber

up
10. arachnid
13. locate

backward
11. place to sit

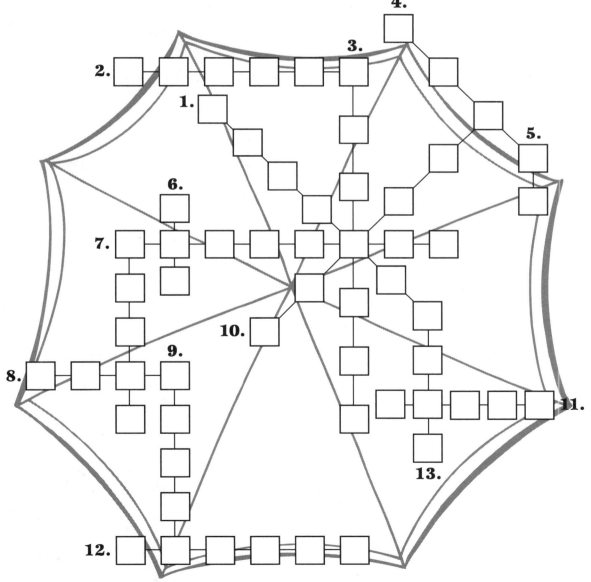

FE11004 © 1999 Fearon Teacher Aids

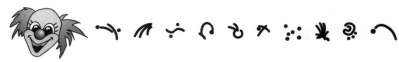

Hey Spooky Spider! Activities

Comparison Charts

Have students use reference materials to make charts listing characteristics of different types of spiders. Write facts about the spiders' appearance, food, homes, activities, and so on. Draw a simple illustration of each spider, cut it out, and glue it to the chart.

More About Spiders

Students can read one of the books listed to the right or another book or poem about spiders. Share the poem or the main idea of the story with the class.

Make a Spooky Spider

Students can make their own "spooky spiders."

Use clay for the body and pipe cleaners for the legs.

Alternative: Cut spiders from construction paper. Decorate with crayons or markers. Punch a hole in the body with a hole punch. Thread string or yarn through the hole and tie a knot to keep it from pulling through.

Use string, yarn, or thread and a large darning needle to weave a web across an empty shoe box. Use a hole punch or make holes with the darning needle while weaving.

Students can use the spiders they made to act out "Hey Spooky Spider!" while they read the poem.

Tell a Tall Tale

Have students write a tall tale about a spider. A tall tale is a story that includes obvious exaggerations: *The spider's legs were so long, it could walk across a football field in two steps.* Illustrate the story and read it to the class.

Related Reading

Charlotte's Web by E. B. White (Harper, 1952).

Miss Spider's Tea Party by David Kirk (Calloway, 1994).

Spiders by Kate Petty (Watts, 1985).

Spiders by Lionel Bender (Gloucester, 1988).

Related Topics

spiders, prey and predators, insects, habitats, webs

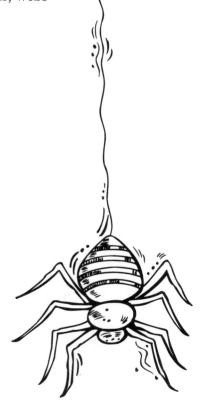

FE11004 © 1999 Fearon Teacher Aids

Let's Sneak a Peek

Options

A   B

A	B	
1	1	Look, quick! Under Mom's bed, A present is hidden from us.
2	2	Look, quick! Under Mom's bed, Try not to make a fuss.
All	1	Let's sneak a peek, And chance a glance, A little view will do.
	2	Let's dare to stare, And try to spy, We will not say we knew.
1	1	Look, quick! Inside the box, I wonder what it will be?
2	2	Look, quick! Inside the box, I wonder what we will see?
All	1	Let's sneak a peek, And chance a glance, A little view will do.
	2	Let's dare to stare, And try to spy, We will not say we knew.
1	1	Look, quick! There is a note, Is it a secret clue?
2	2	Look, quick! Mom wrote the note, It says, "Ha ha, I fooled you!"

FE11004 © 1999 Fearon Teacher Aids

Let's Sneak a Peek Puzzle

Help the children in the poem get a peek at the hidden gift. Follow the directions below to see what the present is.

1. Going from left to right, cross out every third letter.

2. Cross out every letter *b*.

3. Cross out every letter *g*.

4. Draw a circle around letters *w, d, m*.

5. Do not cross out any *y*s.

6. Cross out all vowels except *a, e, i*.

7. Write the remaining letters in order on the spaces below.

The present is ___   __ __ __ __ __ __   __ __ __ __ __ ___ .

Let's Sneak a Peek Activities

What's in the Box?

Have students draw a gift box and decide what might be inside it. They can write a descriptive paragraph describing the object without naming it. Write what the object is on the back of the paper. Have students exchange papers with classmates and read each other's description, then try to identify the object inside the box.

Twenty Questions

Have students place an object inside a box and cover the box with wrapping paper or construction paper. Play Twenty Questions to discover what object is in the box. One student is the leader. Students take turns asking questions about what the leader has in the box. Only questions that can be answered "yes" or "no" may be used.

The leader answers the questions and keeps track of the number of questions asked. Encourage students to ask questions using adjectives to describe the object before they try to guess. For example, a player may ask, "Is the object green?" "Is it round?" The person who guesses the object within Twenty Questions is the winner and becomes the leader for the next game.

Writing Options

Option 1: Have students write about a special gift they have received. Tell who it was from and why it was special.

Option 2: Have students write about a time when they found a hidden present. Have them describe how they felt and what they did about their discovery.

Option 3: Have students write about a special present they would like to buy for someone else. Describe the present, who it is for, what occasion it would be for, and where they would hide it.

X Marks the Spot

Have each student draw a floor plan of a room in his or her home. Place an *X* over every place a present could be hidden.

Related Topics

gifts; birthdays; surprises; discoveries; hiding; character traits like respect, generosity, honesty, and trust

FE11004 © 1999 Fearon Teacher Aids

Manatee Magic

Options
A   B

1	1	Mandy, the magical manatee,
		Shares her magic in the moonlit sea.
	2	She waves her flippers gracefully,
		Granting wishes joyfully.

All   All   Wherever she goes,
Mandy's magic flows,
Deep down to the creatures below.

Bright sunfish glow,
Like glistening snow,
And the starfish all shine in a row.

2	1	Mandy, the magical manatee,
		Shares her magic in the moonlit sea.
	2	One night she set the fishes free,
		Granting their wish to fly from the sea.

All   All   Wherever she goes,
Mandy's magic flows
Now she watches the sky from below.

Bright sunfish glow,
Like glistening snow,
And the starfish all shine in a row.

FE11004 © 1999 Fearon Teacher Aids

Manatee Magic *(cont'd)*

Options
A B

1	1	Mandy, the magical manatee,
		Stares up at the sky nervously.
	2	The fish are flying happy and free,
		Shining and sparkling over the sea.

All All   Wherever she goes,
Mandy's magic flows
Now she watches the sky from below.

Bright sunfish glow,
Like glistening snow,
And the starfish all shine in a row.

2	1	Mandy, the magical manatee,
		Waves her magic flippers gracefully.
	2	She brought the fishes back into the sea.
		To restore nature's peace and harmony.

All All   Wherever she goes,
Mandy's magic flows,
Deep down to the creatures below.

Bright sunfish all glow,
Like glistening snow,
And the starfish all shine in a row.

Manatee Magic Puzzle

In the poem, Mandy watched over the creatures of the sea. Use the pictures to name some creatures that live in water. Write each answer in the space next to the pictures.

1. _____

2. _____

3. _____

4. _____

5. _____

6. _____

7. _____

8. _____

9. _____

10. _____

11. _____

12. _____

13. _____

14. _____

◆ **Bonus:** Draw pictures as symbols for words to write these creatures' names.

15. parrot fish

16. stonefish

17. oarfish

18. butterfish

FE11004 © 1999 Fearon Teacher Aids

Manatee Magic Activities

Manatee Mural

Working in small groups, students can draw or paint large murals on butcher paper or posterboard showing different scenes from the poem. Display the mural on the wall.

Mobile Magic

Students can make a mobile showing the characters from the poem. A mobile can be made from a wire coat hanger or by using a 3-inch (7.5-cm) wide strip of posterboard bent into a circle and attached at the ends, forming a hoop. Punch four holes equally spaced around the circle. Tie two pieces of string across the circle in an "X pattern." To make a hanger for the mobile, tie another piece of string to the place where the two strings cross to form the X.

Students can trace and cut the patterns on the next page or cut and decorate their own shapes to represent the characters in the poem and other sea creatures. Tie yarn or string from the hoop with the figures attached to the ends of the string at various levels. Suspend Mandy, the magical manatee, from the center. Placing Mandy above the fish shows the beginning or ending of the poem when the fish are deep in the ocean. Suspending Mandy below the fish represents the middle of the poem when the fish are flying in the sky.

More About Manatees

Have students use reference materials to look up information about manatees. Have them write a brief report and share the information with the class. Ask them to answer these questions: *How big are manatees? Where do they live? What do they eat?*

Illustrate Elements of Fiction

Have students fold a piece of paper horizontally into six equal sections. Unfold the paper and write the title of the poem, "Manatee Magic," in the top section. Write one heading in each remaining section to depict these elements of fiction: *setting, characters, beginning of plot, middle of plot, ending of plot.* Draw an appropriate illustration in each section.

Related Topics

manatees, oceans, fish, magic, starfish, wishes, sea creatures

Manatee Magic Patterns

16

Mixed-Up Martian

Options		
A	**B**	
1	1	A mixed-up Martian from Mars,
		Came to Earth for spaghetti in jars.
2	2	As he zoomed down the street
		A parade he did meet,
		With a king and three movie stars.
All	3	Instead of confetti
		He threw spaghetti,
		What a big mess that Martian made!
	4	By throwing spaghetti instead of confetti
		He messed up the king's parade.
1	1	Then the mixed-up Martian from Mars,
		Tried to cook spaghetti from jars.
2	2	As he rolled up the meat
		He planned a real treat,
		For the king and the three movie stars.
All	3	But instead of spaghetti
		He cooked the confetti,
		He found at the king's parade.
	4	By cooking confetti instead of spaghetti
		He messed up the meal that he made.
1	1	The mixed-up Martian from Mars,
		Had to head back out to the stars.
2	2	Now all the Martians he meets
		Want what Earthlings don't eat,
	All	Confetti and meatballs in jars.

Mixed-Up Martian Puzzle

The Mixed-Up Martian is back on Earth and is having problems again. Help him find rhyming words in the poem. Write words in each jar that rhyme with the word on the lid. At the bottom of each jar write another rhyming word of your own that doesn't appear in the poem.

1. cars

*

2. fade

*

3. seals

*

4. feet

*

5. dead

*

6. Betty

*

7. be

*

Bonus: The Mixed-Up Martian wrote his letters out of order on his T-shirt. Unscramble the letters to read his message.

tEa
tame;
'sti
a
ratte!

FE11004 © 1999 Fearon Teacher Aids

Mixed-Up Martian Activities

Mixed-Up Martian Play

Students can work together to write a play about another adventure the Mixed-Up Martian might have had on Earth. Write speaking parts for the Martian and other characters in the poem, like the king and the three movie stars, or create new characters. Have students put funny situations in the play that show ways the Martian got mixed up on Earth.

Here are some ideas to get students started. What happened when the Mixed-Up Martian tried to . . .

- . . . drive a car
- . . . milk a cow
- . . . row a boat
- . . . ride an elephant
- . . . plant a garden
- . . . program a VCR
- . . . use a computer
- . . . read a map
- . . . climb a tree

Mixed-Up Martian Puppet

Students can create puppets of the Mixed-Up Martian. The puppet can be made from a sock, a paper bag, or from posterboard taped to a craft stick or drinking straw. Have the Mixed-Up Martian puppet tell about himself and the planet Mars, or tell about one of his mixed-up adventures on Earth.

Television News Report

Ask students to pretend they are television news reporters who were at the king's parade. Have them write the script for a two-minute television news report that tells about the strange creature from Mars, the mix-up that happened at the parade, and the reactions of the people watching the parade.

Life on Mixed-Up Mars

Ask students to imagine a planet as mixed up as the Mixed-Up Martian. Would trees grow upside down? Would Martians walk on the ceiling, swim in the sky, or eat with a screwdriver and pliers? Have students draw a scene from everyday life on the Mixed-Up Martian's mixed-up planet.

Write a Rebus Story

Write the story from the poem in your own words. Choose some nouns in your story and replace those words with pictures. For example, draw a picture of spaghetti in place of the word. Every time the same word is used, draw the same picture instead of writing out the word.

Related Topics

Mars, planets, parades, food, spaghetti, kings

Moody Moon

Options	
A	B

All	1	The moody moon
		Said to silly sun,
1		"Please help me laugh today.
		Today I'm full
		But very soon,
		I fear I'll fade away."
All	2	The silly sun
		Told moody moon,
2		"Please do not whine today.
		You'll change into
		A gibbous moon,*
		Half, quarter, and new phase."
All	1	The moody moon
		Thanked silly sun,
1		"You made me smile today.
		I'll change my looks
		But I'll still be here,
		I won't fade away!"

* A gibbous moon is three-quarters full.

FE11004 © 1999 Fearon Teacher Aids

 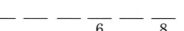 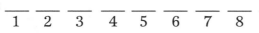

Moody Moon Puzzle

Solve each riddle by unscrambling words from the poem. Then write each numbered letter over the corresponding number in the riddle answer spaces.

Riddle #1: What do you call wild, scary children who live on the moon?

A. nsu   __ __ __
          9

B. dafe   __ __ __ __
               7

C. omon   __ __ __ __
        1   3

D. wen   __ __ __
        4

E. bigsoub   __ __ __ __ __ __ __
                 2   5

F. trqeuar   __ __ __ __ __ __ __
              6   8

Answer: __ __ __ __ __ __ __ __ __
      1 2 3 4 5 6 7 8 9

Riddle #2: What has no wings, yet flies on the moon?

G. guhla   __ __ __ __ __
         2 3   7

H. osklo   __ __ __ __ __
        5   2

I. lafh   __ __ __ __
          6   4

J. lufl   __ __ __ __
        1

Answer: __ . __ . __ .   __ __ __ __
       1   2   3   4 5 6 7

FE11004 © 1999 Fearon Teacher Aids

Reproducible

Moody Moon Puzzle *(cont'd)*

Riddle #3: What was the astronaut's favorite dessert?

K. odoym   ___ ___ ___ ___ ___
                      3

L. lisyl   ___ ___ ___ ___ ___
                 6

M. pasele   ___ ___ ___ ___ ___ ___
                      7

N. nghcea   ___ ___ ___ ___ ___ ___
                              4

O. meils   ___ ___ ___ ___ ___
                 1

P. yatdo   ___ ___ ___ ___ ___
                 2

Q. sheap   ___ ___ ___ ___ ___
             5

Answer: ___ ___ ___ ___   ___ ___ ___
            1   2   3   4   5   6   7

FE11004 © 1999 Fearon Teacher Aids

Moody Moon Activities

Moon Phases

Have students use reference materials to write a report on the phases of the moon and why these changes occur. Include illustrations to show each phase. Label drawings.

Moon Time Line

Students can use what they learned to make a pictorial time line showing the different phases of the moon's cycle. They can label each picture and include the approximate number of days between each phase.

Moon Rhymes

Let students brainstorm a list of words that rhyme with *moon*. Encourage them to think of words with more than one syllable, like *monsoon, balloon,* and *baboon.* Remind students that rhyming words don't always have the same ending letters (*moon* and *June*).

Just So

Read one of the *Just So Stories* by Rudyard Kipling to the class. Many of these stories have been rewritten and illustrated as single books. Ask students to write their own "Just So" stories to explain why the moon has different phases. Their stories should tell what the moon was originally like and what happened to the moon that resulted in changing phases.

More About the Moon

Use this poem as an introduction to a unit on the solar system. Have students read another book or poem about the moon, space travel, our solar system, or the universe. Have them share the poems with the class or give a summary of the book.

What If?

- What if the moon were made of green cheese?

- What if there was really a man in the moon?

- What if people could live on the moon?

- What if Earth had more than one moon?

Encourage students to write "what if" questions about the moon, then answer the questions with a story, poem, or illustration.

Moon Journal

Have students make moon journals. Start on the first day of a full moon. Each night, ask students to look at the moon and draw a picture of how it looks. If the moon is not visible, they can write what weather conditions prevented them from seeing the moon. Continue the journal for 28 days to include one full cycle.

FE11004 © 1999 Fearon Teacher Aids

Moody Moon Activities *(cont'd)*

Moon Facts

Have students use reference materials to find fun facts about the moon. *How far away is it? How large is it? How much does it weigh? How much would a 100-pound person weigh on the moon?* Have students write their fun facts on paper circles and display them on a bulletin board.

Moon Math

Have students use the moon facts they learned to write moon math story problems. For example: *On the average, the moon is 238,860 miles away from Earth. If we could drive to the moon, how many hours would it take at 55 miles per hour?* Have students trade moon math problems with classmates and solve them.

Related Reading

The Beginning of the Armadilloes, The Butterfly That Stamped, The Cat That Walked by Himself, and *The Crab That Played with the Sea* by Rudyard Kipling, illustrated by Charles Keeping (Bedrick, 1983).

Just So Stories by Rudyard Kipling, illustrated by J. M. Gleason (Smith, 1946).

Just So Stories by Rudyard Kipling, illustrated by Michael Foreman (Viking, 1987).

Just So Stories by Rudyard Kipling, illustrated by Safaya Salter (Holt, 1987).

Many Moons by James Thurber (Harcourt, 1945).

Moon Man by Tomi Ungerer (Harper, 1967).

The Moon Seems to Change by Franklyn Bradley (Harper, 1987).

Related Topics

moon, sun, solar system, astronauts, space program, phases

Mud Pie, Moon Pie

Options

A   B

A	B	
1	1	There were many pies at the county fair,
		Apple, pumpkin, blueberry, and pear,
2		Peach, banana, and chocolate eclair,
	All	But Granny's pie was the best one there.
All	2	It was a mud pie, a moon pie,
		She filled it with a big surprise,
	All	And no one there could believe their eyes,
		When Granny's pie began to fly.
1	1	There were many pies at the county fair,
		Apple, pumpkin, blueberry, and pear,
2	All	Peach, banana, and chocolate eclair,
		But Granny's pie flew up in the air.

1st PRIZE

FE11004 © 1999 Fearon Teacher Aids

Reproducible

Mud Pie, Moon Pie *(cont'd)*

| All | 2 | It was a mud pie, a moon pie,
She filled it with a big surprise, |
| | All | And no one there could believe their eyes,
When Granny's pie fell from the sky. |

| 1 | 1 | There were many pies at the county fair,
Apple, pumpkin, blueberry, and pear, |
| 2 | | Peach, banana, and chocolate eclair,
But Granny's pie was the lightest one there. |

| All | 2 | It was a mud pie, a moon pie,
She filled it with a big surprise, |
| | All | And no one there could believe their eyes,
When Granny's pie won first prize. |

FE11004 © 1999 Fearon Teacher Aids

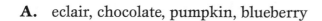

Mud Pie, Moon Pie Puzzle

Write each list of words in alphabetical order. Then write each numbered letter in the pie to spell a type of pie.

A. eclair, chocolate, pumpkin, blueberry

— — — — — — — — —
     6

— — — — — — — —
1   4   2   7

— — — — —
  3

— — — — — — —
       5

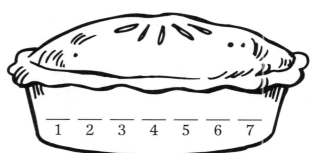

1 2 3 4 5 6 7

B. their, best, first, county, lightest

— — — — —
  3

— — — — —
1   6

— — — — —
   4

— — — — — —
    2

— — — — —
   5

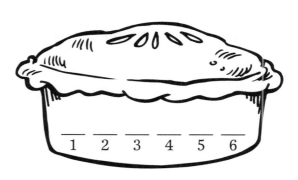

1 2 3 4 5 6

FE11004 © 1999 Fearon Teacher Aids

Reproducible

Mud Pie, Moon Pie Puzzle *(cont'd)*

C. first, won, apple, surprise, Granny, banana

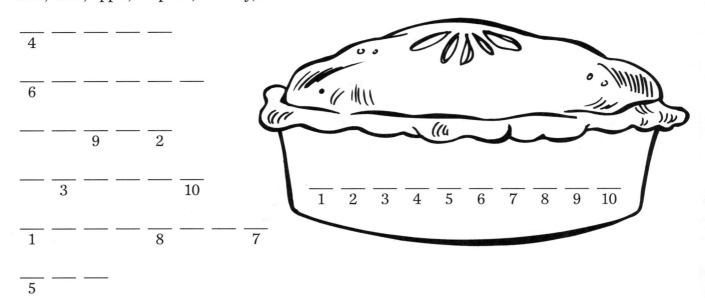

$\overline{}_4 \ \overline{} \ \overline{} \ \overline{} \ \overline{}$

$\overline{}_6 \ \overline{} \ \overline{} \ \overline{} \ \overline{} \ \overline{}$

$\overline{} \ \overline{} \ \overline{}_9 \ \overline{} \ \overline{}_2$

$\overline{} \ \overline{}_3 \ \overline{} \ \overline{} \ \overline{}_{10}$

$\overline{}_1 \ \overline{} \ \overline{} \ \overline{}_8 \ \overline{} \ \overline{}_7$

$\overline{}_5 \ \overline{} \ \overline{}$

D. prize, pie, peach, pumpkin, pear

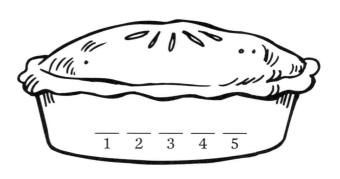

$\overline{} \ \overline{} \ \overline{} \ \overline{}_3 \ \overline{}$

$\overline{} \ \overline{} \ \overline{}_4 \ \overline{}$

$\overline{} \ \overline{}_2 \ \overline{}$

$\overline{}_1 \ \overline{} \ \overline{} \ \overline{}$

$\overline{} \ \overline{} \ \overline{} \ \overline{} \ \overline{} \ \overline{} \ \overline{}_5$

FE11004 © 1999 Fearon Teacher Aids

Mud Pie, Moon Pie Activities

Surprise Pie

Students can write a recipe for making Granny's pie on a recipe card or 3" x 5" (7.5 cm x 12.5 cm) index card. Have them use their imaginations as they list the ingredients. Be sure to include directions for how to make this pie.

Class Cookbook

Combine students' recipes for Granny's pie. Invite students to write recipes for other made-up treats (like Confetti and Meatballs). Photocopy and make a class cookbook.

No-Bake Mini Pumpkin Pies

Try this recipe for no-bake mini pumpkin pies with the class.

1. Mix crushed graham crackers with soft butter or margarine.

2. Pat into cupcake liners.

3. Prepare one small box of instant vanilla pudding according to package directions.

4. Add one 16-ounce can of pumpkin pie filling.

5. Mix thoroughly.

6. Spoon mixture into prepared cupcake cups.

7. Top with whipped cream.

County Fair

Have students design a menu listing many items that could be sold at a county fair. Have them include the items under different headings, like *desserts, vegetables, fruits, sandwiches*, and *snacks*. Include illustrations and prices. Remind them that besides Granny's Mud Pie, Moon Pie, they can create their own unusual items to include on the menu.

Interview the Spectators

Ask students to imagine they will interview someone who was at the county fair. To prepare, have them write at least six questions about what happened to Granny's pie and what that person's reaction was. Remind them to use the six question words *who, what, when, where, why,* and *how*. After the questions are listed, students can write the responses of the imaginary person interviewed.

Alternative: After students write their interview questions, have them trade papers with a classmate. Ask them to imagine they are the person being interviewed and write the answers.

What a Surprise!

Many of the words that rhyme with *surprise* do not end with the letters *-ise*. Some end in *-ies*, like *pies* and *spies*. *Prize* ends in *-ize*. Make headings for each ending on chart paper. Have students brainstorm a list of rhyming words under each heading.

FE11004 © 1999 Fearon Teacher Aids

Mud Pie, Moon Pie Activities (cont'd)

County Fair Mural

Working in small groups, have students design and draw a mural portraying the county fair and the events that happened in the poem. Display the mural on the wall or bulletin board.

Sing a Song of Sixpence

Read the first verse of the nursery rhyme "Sing a Song of Sixpence" to the class. When that pie was opened, the birds began to sing. Ask students to write or draw what they think happened when Granny's pie was opened.

At the Fair

Many words rhyme with *fair*. Ask students to list rhyming words, then use the words to write a short poem titled "At the Fair." Students can add illustrations.

Related Reading

Charlotte's Web by E. B. White (Harper, 1952).

Pickle in the Middle and Other Easy Snacks by Frances Zweifel (Harper, 1979).

Quick and Easy Cookbook by Robyn Supraner (Troll, 1981).

The State Fair Book by Jack Pierce (Carolrhoda, 1980).

The Storybook Cookbook by Carol MacGregor (Prentice, 1967).

Related Topics

pies, fairs, grandparents, desserts, fruit, contests, prizes

FE11004 © 1999 Fearon Teacher Aids

Oh Brother!

Options		
A	**B**	
1	1	Hurry! Hurry! Call the judge.
		Little brother is holding a grudge.
2		He won't play and he won't budge.
		All I did was give him a nudge.
All	All	Oh brother!
1	2	Hurry! Hurry! Call the judge.
		Little brother is holding a grudge.
2		He's so stubborn, he won't budge.
		I think I'll bribe him with some fudge.
All	All	Oh brother!
1	3	Hurry! Hurry! Call the judge.
		Little brother ate my fudge.
2		His hands are messy, and with a grudge,
		He wiped his hands and left a smudge.
All	All	Oh brother!
1	4	Hurry! Hurry! Call the judge.
		Little brother is holding a grudge.
2		He still won't play, he ate my fudge,
		And I was blamed for the chocolate smudge.
All	All	Oh brother! Oh brother!

FE11004 © 1999 Fearon Teacher Aids

Oh Brother! Puzzle

Fill in the blocks using words from the poem. The first letter of each word is given.

1. j
2. l
3. b
4. h
5. g
6. c
7. h
8. f
9. p
10. o
11. w
12. a
13. s
14. s
15. h
16. b
17.
18. b

FE11004 © 1999 Fearon Teacher Aids

Oh Brother! Activities

In Your Own Words

Ask students to write what happened in "Oh Brother!" in their own words. Discuss *synonyms* (words that have the same, or nearly the same meaning). Encourage students to replace some words from the poem with synonyms. Use this opportunity to introduce or review use of a thesaurus.

Cartoon Creations

Have students divide a sheet of paper into four equal sections. In each section, have them draw a cartoon showing one verse of the poem.

Oh Brother! Oh Sister!

Have students write a paragraph about a time when their brother, sister, cousin, or friend did something for which they were blamed. Have them add a moral to the end of the story explaining why it is important for brothers and sisters (cousins, friends, classmates, and so on) to get along together.

Family Fun

Ask students to draw pictures of themselves and a brother, sister, cousin, or friend doing something fun together. They can write captions for their pictures.

Sibling Survey

Have students work together to conduct surveys about brothers and sisters. Each student could tally the responses for one question. Survey questions could include: *How many students have no brothers or sisters? How many have both brothers and sisters? sisters only? brothers only? older brothers? younger brothers? older sisters? younger sisters?* Combine responses to make class graphs or charts to display the results.

Related Reading

Backyard Angel by Judy Delton (Houghton, 1983).

Fudge, Superfudge (1980), and *Tales of a Fourth Grade Nothing* by Judy Blume (Dutton, 1972).

Secrets of a Small Brother by Richard Margolis (Macmillan, 1984).

Related Topics

brothers, sisters, families, cooperation, fudge, messes, tattling

FE11004 © 1999 Fearon Teacher Aids

Orange Tennis Shoes

Options
A   B

All	1	Hear ye! Hear ye!
		Did you hear the news?
1	2	Cows down in the pasture,
		Are wearin' orange tennis shoes.
All	1	Hear ye! Hear ye!
		This bet you will not lose.
2	2	Cows are runnin' up the hill,
		Wearin' orange tennis shoes.
All	1	Hear ye! Hear ye!
		This isn't April Fool's!
1	2	Cow's milk's turnin' to juice,
		From wearin' orange tennis shoes.
All	1	Hear ye! Hear ye!
		Our town has made the news.
2	2	Now everyone's drinkin' orange juice,
		And wearin' orange tennis shoes.

FE11004 © 1999 Fearon Teacher Aids

Orange Tennis Shoes Puzzle

After giving orange juice, the cows started wearing different-colored tennis shoes—red, pink, purple, and yellow. To discover the kinds of juice the cows gave, change words from the poem by following the directions. Write the type of juice in the space.

Word	Directions
1. m a d e	change *d* to *p* take off *m* add *gr* at the beginning

Juice: _____

2. t e n n i s	change *t* to *l* add *mo* after *e* take off *nis*

Juice: _____

3. p a s t u r e	change *p* to *c* change *s* to r take off *ure* add *ro* before *t*

Juice: _____

4. o r a n g e	change *r* to *m* add *t* at the beginning take off *nge* add *to* at the end

Juice: _____

5. w e a r i n g	take off *ing* change *w* to *p*

Juice: _____

Word	Directions
6. m a d e	take off *m* change *d* to *pp* add *l* before *e*

Juice: _____

7. r u n n i n g	take off *ing* add *p* to the beginning change last *n* to *e*

Juice: _____

8. a p r i l	add *ef* before *r* add *u* after *r* add *gr* at the beginning change *l* to *t*

Juice: _____

9. e v e r y o n e	take off *one* change first *e* to *st* add *r* before *y* change *v* to *b* add *raw* after *t*

Juice: _____

10. m i l k	add *ne* after *i* change *m* to *p* change *k* to *e* add *app* before *l*

Juice: _____

FE11004 © 1999 Fearon Teacher Aids

Orange Tennis Shoes Activities

Send a Postcard

Ask students to imagine they are on vacation in the town where everyone, including cows, wears orange tennis shoes. Write a postcard to a friend describing what happened to cause this event. On the front of the postcard, draw a picture showing cows wearing orange tennis shoes.

Orange Day

Make up a new holiday called Orange Day. Let students create decorations from orange construction paper and crepe paper. Include several "orange" activities. Some suggestions are:

- Invite students to wear as many orange items of clothing as possible.

- Mix red and yellow paint to make orange. Have a finger-painting contest.

- Celebrate with orange juice, carrot sticks, orange gelatin, oranges, and other orange treats.

- Squeeze your own orange juice.

- Have students make a list of items that are orange. Have them compare their list with a friend's to see who thought of the most items.

- Have an orange riddle contest. Invite students to make up orange riddles and tell them to the class.

Presenting the Orange Tennis Shoe Town

Have students create travel posters or brochures to attract tourists to the town where cows wear orange tennis shoes and give orange juice instead of milk. Use illustrations and text to explain why the town is special.

Make a Book

Have students make books to show what happened in the poem. They can retell the poem in their own words and include an explanation of why the cows started wearing orange tennis shoes and giving orange juice. Illustrate the books.

Related Reading

Oranges by Rogow Zack (Watts, 1988).

A Picture Book of Cows by Dorothy Hinshaw Patent (Holiday, 1982).

Related Topics

cows, shoes, communities, towns, beverages, news

FE11004 © 1999 Fearon Teacher Aids

Pop!

Options		
A	**B**	
1	1	I wanted a balloon, A big one too!
	2	So I bought a red one, And I blew and blew.
All	All	I blew and I blew, And I could not stop. I blew, blew, blew, 'Til the balloon went pop!
2	1	I like to blow bubbles, Some big ones too!
	2	So I bought bubble gum, And I chewed and blew.
All	All	I blew and I blew, And I could not stop. I blew, blew, blew, 'Til the bubble went pop!

(Yuck! There's gum all over my nose!)

Pop! Puzzle

Burst the balloons by unscrambling the letters to make words from the poem. Write each word in the balloon.

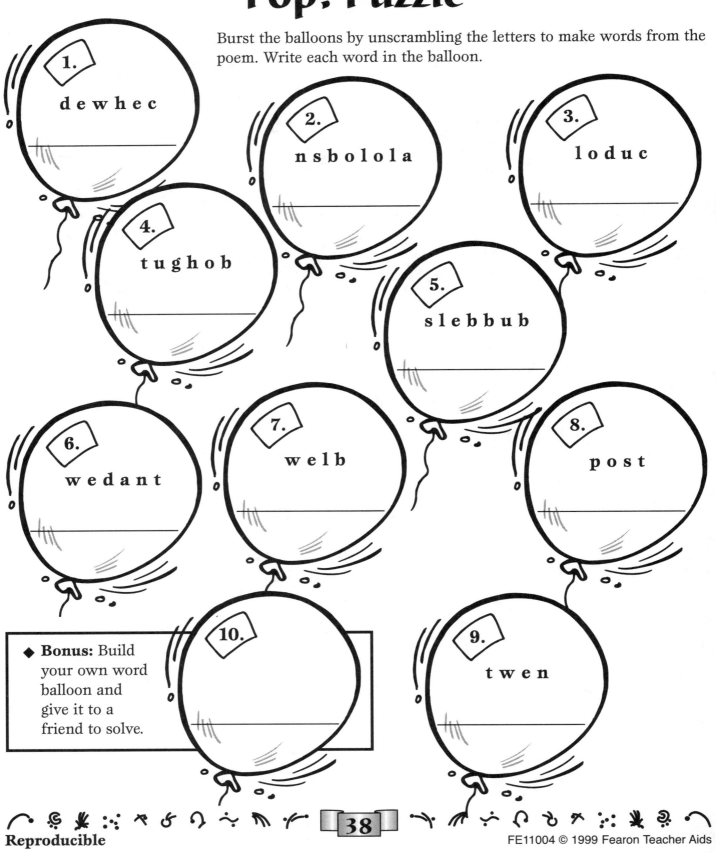

1. d e w h e c

2. n s b o l o l a

3. l o d u c

4. t u g h o b

5. s l e b b u b

6. w e d a n t

7. w e l b

8. p o s t

9. t w e n

10.

◆ **Bonus:** Build your own word balloon and give it to a friend to solve.

FE11004 © 1999 Fearon Teacher Aids

Pop! Activities

Design an Ad

Have students make posters advertising magic bubble gum or balloons. Have them draw pictures of the new product, give it a name, and tell what makes this product so special.

Balloon Creatures

Students can create balloon creatures by blowing up balloons and decorating them. They can make balloon creatures by taping on construction-paper features and decorating with paints or markers. Encourage students to be as creative as possible to make truly unique creatures.

Be careful so the balloons don't pop!

Magic Balloon Stories

After creating balloon creatures, students can write stories about the special or magical things they can do. Let students share balloon creatures and stories with the class.

Alternate Story: Have students write a story about magic bubble gum. Have them tell what magical things happen when bubbles are blown. They can illustrate their stories.

Onomatopoeia

Explain the word *onomatopoeia* (a word that imitates the sound of what is represented). Give several examples: *Cows moo, owls whooo, trains choo-choo.* As a class, brainstorm words that make loud or sudden sounds. For example, things that go *bang! pop! crash! smack!* or *thud!* Make a chart listing the items and sounds they make.

Bubble Contest

Let students have a contest to see who can blow the biggest bubble. It would be a good idea to provide a trash bag and some wet paper towels in case a few bubbles do go "pop!"

Blew and *Blue*

Blew and *blue* are *homonyms* (words that sound the same, but are spelled differently). Challenge students to list as many pairs of homonyms as possible.

Related Topics

sounds, balloons, bubble gum, parties, mouths

FE11004 © 1999 Fearon Teacher Aids

Rappin' Rabbit

Options		
A	**B**	
1	1	Have you seen a rabbit that's red, Wearing a blue cap on his head?
	2	When he puts on that blue cap, That is when he starts to rap.
All	All	He's cool! He's red! He wears a blue cap on his head. Rap, rap! Rap, rabbit! Rappin' Rabbit, rap, rap!
2	1	Rappin' Rabbit is very cool. He learned to rap at rabbit rap school.
	2	When you want to have some fun, Call Rappin' Rabbit, he is the one.
All	All	He's cool! He's red! He wears a blue cap on his head. Rap, rap! Rap, rabbit! Rappin' Rabbit, rap, rap!
3	1	Rappin' Rabbit is cool with raps. When he raps, everyone claps.
	2	People dance and people sing, When Rappin' Rabbit does his thing.
All	All	He's cool! He's red! He wears a blue cap on his head. Rap, rap! Rap, rabbit! Rappin' rabbit, rap, rap!

FE11004 © 1999 Fearon Teacher Aids

Rappin' Rabbit Puzzle

What are Rappin' Rabbit's favorite rap tunes? To find out, choose words from the Word Bank that rhyme with the clue words next to each number. Rewrite the new words in the same order on each CD to name the rap tunes.

Word Bank

Chomp, Hop, Hare, Cool, Carrot, Race, Rap, No, Rappin', Red, Rabbit, Blue, Bunny, Happy, Hat, Real, Wild, Trap (use trap only once with second tune)

1. true bat slap

2. so lap tap

3. head nap face

4. happen top mop

5. parrot stomp map

6. child habit lap

7. snappy care crop nap

8. meal tool funny zap

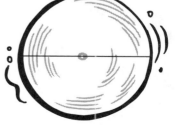

Rappin' Rabbit Activities

Rappin' Rabbit T-shirt

Students can design a Rappin' Rabbit T-shirt. They can draw an outline of a T-shirt shape on a large piece of paper and add the design inside the outline, or draw designs on a real T-shirt using permanent markers. Add a Rappin' Rabbit slogan or saying on the shirt. Before drawing on a real T-shirt, encourage students to draft their ideas on paper.

Rappin' Rabbit Cartoon

Students can create a comic strip about Rappin' Rabbit. They can write a short story about one of his adventures and write it in comic-strip format. Create characters to include in the story.

Rappin' Rabbit for Rent

Have students design a magazine or newspaper ad for Rappin' Rabbit's business of entertaining at parties. Include his qualifications and explain why he would make a party lots of fun.

Music Survey

Take a poll in class to find out what type of music students like best. Have students conduct a survey asking friends and family members about their favorite style of music. Students can prepare charts to show their survey results.

Oldies, but Goodies

Have students ask older family members what kind of music was popular when they were in school. Encourage them to bring in a tape or CD with a sample of this type of music to share with the class.

Write a Rap

Have students work together in small groups to write and perform a rap for the class. Encourage them to select a theme first, then make a list of words that rhyme to use in their raps.

Alternate Rap: Instead of writing an original rap, students could use familiar poems or nursery rhymes and rewrite them as raps. Have them retitle the poems and present them to the class.

Related Topics

rap music, dance, rabbits, rodents, music styles, fads, parties

Cuckoo Time

Options
A B

motions

A	B		
1	1	Please stand up,	(clap clap)
2		Please sit down,	(clap clap)
1	2	Do not act,	(clap clap)
2		Like a clown.	(clap clap)
1	1	Shake your head,	(clap clap)
2		Slap your knee,	(clap clap)
1	2	Do not act,	(clap clap)
2		So crazy.	(clap clap)
1	1	Open your eyes,	(clap clap)
2		Close them shut,	(clap clap)
1	2	Do not act,	(clap clap)
2		Like a nut.	(clap clap)
1	1	Who does this?	(clap clap)
2		We all do,	(clap clap)
1	2	When we act,	(clap clap)
2		Like a cuckoo.	(clap clap)

Cuckoo Time Puzzle

What time is it when your cuckoo calls 13 times?

To find the answer, write each group of words from the poem in alphabetical order. Then write each numbered letter over the corresponding number in the answer space.

1. time   this   them   eyes

___ ___ ___ ___
    8

___ ___ ___ ___
        3

___ ___ ___ ___

___ ___ ___ ___
    2

2. head   does   open   like

___ ___ ___ ___
      15

___ ___ ___ ___

___ ___ ___ ___

___ ___ ___ ___
    6

3. stand   shut   shake   slap

___ ___ ___ ___ ___
      17

___ ___ ___ ___
   7

___ ___ ___ ___ ___

___ ___ ___ ___ ___
   9

4. clock   crazy   clown   close

___ ___ ___ ___ ___

___ ___ ___ ___ ___
  13

___ ___ ___ ___ ___
    14

___ ___ ___ ___ ___

FE11004 © 1999 Fearon Teacher Aids

Cuckoo Time Puzzle *(cont'd)*

5. when knee who nut sit

___ ___ ___ ___
　　　　　　　4

___ ___ ___
___

___ ___ ___
　　　1

___ ___ ___ ___
12

___ ___ ___

6. please cuckoo shut down

___ ___ ___ ___ ___ ___
　　　16

___ ___ ___ ___
　　　10

___ ___ ___ ___ ___ ___
　　　　　　　　　11

___ ___ ___ ___
　　　5

Answer:

___ ___ ___ ___ 　 ___ ___ 　 $\overset{b}{\rule{1em}{0.4pt}}$ ___ ___
1   2   3   4   　5   6   　　　7   8

___ 　 ___ ___ ___ 　 ___ ___ ___ ___ ___!
9   　10 11 12 　13 14 15 16 17

FE11004 © 1999 Fearon Teacher Aids

Cuckoo Time Activities

More Cuckoo Verses

Have students use the same rhyme scheme and rhythm to write additional verses for the poem. Have them include motions like stomping, clicking fingers, or waving hands. Students can share their new verses with the class, taking turns being the leader.

Simon Says

Ask students to invent a game that requires participants to follow directions, like "Simon Says." Ask students to teach the class how to play the game.

Make Clown Masks

Students can make clown masks from paper plates. Have them cut out eye and nose holes, and decorate the back side of the plate with a clown face. Add yarn or construction-paper scraps for hair. Punch a hole on each side of the plate. Tie a 12-inch (30-cm) string to each side to hold the mask in place.

Up, Down, Sit, Stand

Words that mean the opposite are called *antonyms*. Students can write antonyms for words in the poem, then make a list of at least 25 other antonyms.

Map It

Have students write directions on how to get from their classroom to another room in the school. Have them write the destination on another sheet of paper. Remind students that directions must be precise. Have students trade papers with a classmate and follow the directions. If the destination cannot be determined or is incorrect, students should rewrite their directions.

Memory Game

Students can work in small groups to draw illustrations showing each action in the poem on 3" x 5" (7.5 cm x 12.5 cm) index cards (*stand, sit, open eyes*, and so on). Make two cards for each action. Have them make two cards for nouns used in the poem also (*clown, nut*, and so on). When the cards are finished, each group can play a memory game.

Shuffle the cards. Turn all cards face down. The first player turns up two cards. If the cards match, the player keeps the pair and takes another turn. If the cards do not match, the player turns them face down and the next player takes a turn.

Related Topics

games, following directions, rules, noises, movements

FE11004 © 1999 Fearon Teacher Aids

Saguaro Cactus

(suh-GWAH-row)

Options
A B

1	1	In the hot Sonoran Desert
		With its dry and dusty air,
2		Lives a tall saguaro cactus
		And his friend, the prickly pear.

All	All	"Look out, watch out!
		Don't get too close to us.
		Look out, watch out!"
		Warns saguaro cactus.

1	2	The tall saguaro cactus
		Holds two arms up in the air,
2		He watches over the desert
		With his friend, the prickly pear.

FE11004 © 1999 Fearon Teacher Aids

Saguaro Cactus *(cont'd)*

All   All   "Look out, watch out!
                     Don't get too close to us.
                     Look out, watch out!"
                     Warns saguaro cactus.

1   3   The tall saguaro cactus
                     Grows sharp spines everywhere.
2   They help to protect him
                     And his friend, the prickly pear.

All   All   "Look out, watch out!
                     Don't get too close to us.
                     Look out, watch out!"
                     Warns saguaro cactus.

1   4   In the hot Sonoran Desert,
                     If you're hiking, please beware.
2   Don't sit on saguaro cactus
                     Or his friend, the prickly pear.

All   All   Ouch! Ouch!

FE11004 © 1999 Fearon Teacher Aids

Saguaro Cactus Facts

Read the information about the saguaro cactus below. Then turn to the next page for the rest of the activity.

The Sonoran Desert is a hot, low desert covering a section of southwestern Arizona, southeastern California, and northwestern Mexico. This desert is the only place where the gigantic saguaro cactus grows naturally. Saguaros survive in this dry desert because they absorb large amounts of water even when very little rain falls, and store it for use in the dry months.

A full-grown saguaro cactus is over 35 feet (10.5 m) tall and weighs many tons. A saguaro can live up to 250 years, but grows very slowly. It takes a saguaro about 25 years to grow 12 inches (30 cm). Saguaros begin to grow their arms when they are over 12 feet (3.5 m) tall, and are between 75 and 100 years old. No two saguaros look the same. While some grow straight, others grow in a twisted manner. The number and position of the arms also vary. Some saguaros only grow two or three arms, while others grow more than ten. Saguaro cacti are covered with sharp, needle-like spines that protect them from thirsty animals, provide shade for themselves from the scorching sun, and act as barriers against the desert wind.

Even though they have sharp spines, the saguaro cactus provides homes for several different types of desert birds. Gila woodpeckers peck holes into the cactus. Once a hole is created, other birds move in. White-wing doves pollinate the plant while feeding on the nectar in the blossoms at the top of the cactus. The saguaro then produces a fruit. It has a green oval peeling that covers a bright red, sweet pulp containing many tiny, black seeds. Not only is this delicious fruit eaten by desert animals and insects, it also has been harvested for centuries by Native Americans of the area to make syrup and jam. Thus, the giant saguaros live in harmony with other desert plants and creatures by providing shade, shelter, and food.

Helms, Christopher L. *Sonoran Desert: The Story Behind Scenery*. KC Publications, Inc. 1980, 18–23.

Saguaro Cactus Puzzle

Use the symbols in the key to write words from the text and poem. Each letter in the key has a symbol created by the shape of the lines around it. Write the corresponding letter below the symbol that represents it. Then write the letters for each word in reverse order, from back to front, to decode the words.

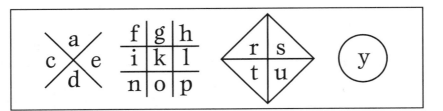

Key:

X (a c e d)	Tic-tac-toe grid	Diamond (r s t u)	Circle
a / c e / d	f g h / i k l / n o p	r s / t u	y

1. △ ⊓ ⊓ L

   _ _ _ _
   _____

2. ◥ ◢ ◣ < ∨ <

   _ _ _ _ _ _
   _____

3. ○ ◤ ∧

   _ _ _
   _____

4. ⊓ ◤ ∨ ◢ ⊔ ∨ ◥

   _ _ _ _ _ _ _
   _____

5. ◣ ∨ > L

   _ _ _ _
   _____

6. ◣ ◤ > ◥ > ∧

   _ _ _ _ _ _
   _____

Saguaro Cactus Puzzle *(cont'd)*

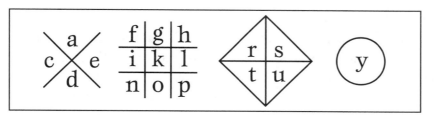

7. ⌐ ⟩ ▽ ⊓

    — — — — —

    ——————

8. ⌐ ⋁ ◿ ⊓ ⌐ ⊓ ◺

    — — — — — — —

    ———————————

9. ⌈ ◿ ⋁ ⌐ ◺

    — — — — —

    ——————

10. ◯ ⌐ ▢ ⟩ ⌐ ◿ ⌈

    — — — — — — —

    ————————

11. ◺ ⟨ ⌐ ⌐ ⌈ ◺

    — — — — — —

    ——————

12. ⋀ ⌐ ⟨ ⌐ ◿ ⌐

    — — — — — —

    ——————

FE11004 © 1999 Fearon Teacher Aids

Reproducible

Saguaro Cactus Activities

Make Your Own Cactus

Have students use reference materials to find photographs of saguaro cacti and prickly pears. They can use clay to make models of the cactus and prickly pear. Toothpicks painted green will work for cactus spines.

Other Types of Cacti

Have students use reference materials to write a report about another type of cactus and where it grows. Have students include illustrations of the type of cactus they researched.

Compare and Contrast

Have students use the information given about the saguaro cactus and the material they found about another type of cactus to compare and contrast the two types of cacti.

If Cacti Could Talk

Ask students to imagine themselves as a saguaro or other type of cactus. Have them write a short speech the cactus might give if it could talk. Be sure the speech includes information about the beauty and dangers of the desert. Have students give their cactus speeches to the class.

Map It

Have students use reference materials to show the location of the Sonoran Desert on a blank map of North America. Have them find and label two other North American deserts and the states and/or countries where they are located.

Related Reading

Cactus by Cynthia Overbeck (Lerner, 1982).

Cactus in the Desert by Phyllis S. Busch (Harper, 1979).

Desert Giant: The World of the Saguaro Cactus by Barbara Bash (Little, 1989).

Desert Voices by Byrd Baylor (Macmillan, 1981).

Deserts by Clive Catchpole (Dial, 1984).

The 100-Year-Old Cactus by Anita Holmes (Raintree, 1979).

Related Topics

cactus, deserts, Sonoran Desert, plants, southwest, Native Americans

FE11004 © 1999 Fearon Teacher Aids

Snapdragon Fly

Options

A   B

1	All	A snippy snappy snapdragon Once met a dragonfly.
	1	Begged the snippy snappy snapdragon, "Please teach me how to fly."
2	All	"You silly snappy snapdragon," The dragonfly replied.
	2	"You are rooted to the ground And you'll never touch the sky."
1	All	The snippy snappy snapdragon Snapped at the dragonfly,
	1	"I will hang onto your wing To fly high and touch the sky."
All	All	But the snippy snappy snapdragon Was rooted to the ground.
	2	That snippy snappy snapdragon Pulled the dragonfly right down.
2	All	"You silly snappy snapdragon, Just look what you have done.
	1	My wing is bent and broken Now I'll never reach the sun."
All	All	Now the snippy snappy snapdragon Is home to the dragonfly.
	2	They wait for snippy snappy To grow tall and touch the sky.

FE11004 © 1999 Fearon Teacher Aids

Reproducible

Snapdragon Fly Puzzle

Use the secret code to find the words from the poem. First, decipher the code by writing the letter that comes right before it in the alphabet. Then use the code to write the words. Write the numbered letters in order to answer the riddle.

a	z	h	_____	o	_____	v	_____
b	a	i	_____	p	_____	w	_____
c	_____	j	_____	q	_____	x	_____
d	_____	k	_____	r	_____	y	_____
e	_____	l	_____	s	_____	z	_____
f	_____	m	_____	t	_____		
g	_____	n	_____	u	_____		

1. g m z ___ ___ ___
                14

2. e s b h p o ___ ___ ___ ___ ___ ___
                        4

3. t v o ___ ___ ___
         2

4. u f b d i ___ ___ ___ ___ ___
                13

5. x j o h ___ ___ ___ ___
                    8

6. h s p v o e ___ ___ ___ ___ ___ ___
                            11

7. t o b q ___ ___ ___ ___
                    6

8. q v m m f e ___ ___ ___ ___ ___ ___
                    5

9. e p x o ___ ___ ___ ___
                    3

10. t j m m z ___ ___ ___ ___ ___
                    7

11. i p n f ___ ___ ___ ___
                        15

12. u p v d i ___ ___ ___ ___ ___
                 10

13. u b m m ___ ___ ___ ___
                 1

14. c s p l f o ___ ___ ___ ___ ___ ___
                        12

15. h s p x ___ ___ ___ ___
         9

Question: What reptile is the snippy snappy snapdragon's best friend?

Answer: ___ ___ ___ ___ ___ ___ ___ ___ ___ ___   ___ ___ ___ ___ ___ ___
          1   2 3 4 5 6 7 8 9   10 11 12 13 14 15

FE11004 © 1999 Fearon Teacher Aids

Snapdragon Fly Activities

Grow Your Own Snapdragons

Let students plant snapdragon seeds in empty cottage cheese or other type plastic containers. They can cover the outside of the containers with construction paper decorated with drawings of dragonflies. Have students write their names on the bottoms of the containers.

Use about an inch (2.5 cm) of loose gravel and four inches (10 cm) of potting soil in each container. Plant seeds as directed on the package. Let stand on a sunny windowsill. Water lightly every few days to keep soil slightly moist. Have students measure and record the growth of their snapdragon plants on charts. If plants get too large, tie plants gently to stakes made from unsharpened pencils.

First, Second, Third

Have students reread the poem, noting the sequence of events. They can draw a picture time line depicting what happened in each verse. Add a short caption under each illustration.

Then What?

Have students draw a picture that shows what could have happened next to the snapdragon and the dragonfly. Did they grow up towards the sky together, or did something unexpected happen?

Alliteration

Alliteration is the use of several words that begin with the same letter or sound, like *snippy snappy snapdragon*. Have students write the following words in one column on a sheet of paper:

blue	brown	deep
eager	friendly	green
happy	jolly	murky
purple	red	silly
tall	very	zippy

Following each word, have students write three or more alliterative words. Have them use one group of alliterative words to write a two-line poem.

Related Reading

Dragonflies by Cynthia Overbeck (Lerner, 1982).

The Dragonfly Over the Water by Christopher O'Toole (Stevens, 1988).

The World of Dragonflies by Virginia Harrison (Stevens, 1988).

Related Topics

dragonflies, insects, snapdragons, plants, gardens, cooperation

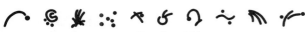 

Snapdragon and Dragonfly Patterns

Use the dragonfly and snapdragon patterns to create reading-record bulletin board designs. After reading a book, students can write the title and author on a dragonfly or snapdragon shape, decorate it, and add it to the Snapdragon Garden of Reading.

FE11004 © 1999 Fearon Teacher Aids

Sneaky Snail

Options

A	B	
1	All	A sneaky snail went snooping, Through my garden late one night,
2	1	To find some juicy melons. He sneaked in to snitch a bite.
3	All	A sneaky snail went snooping, Through my garden late one night.
4	2	But what that sneaky snail saw, Gave him a terrible fright.
1	All	A sneaky snail went snooping, Through my garden late one night.
2	3	He saw a melon dancing, In the soft moonlight.
3	All	A sneaky snail went snooping, Through my garden late one night.
4	4	He heard the melon calling, "Come here and try a bite."
1	All	A sneaky snail went snooping, Through my garden late one night,
2	1 & 3	To taste some juicy melons, But he never snitched a bite.
3	All	A sneaky snail went snooping, Through my garden late one night.
4	2 & 4	There's a dancing melon smiling, But no sneaky snail's in sight.

FE11004 © 1999 Fearon Teacher Aids

Sneaky Snail Puzzle

Help Sneaky Snail get to the melon patch by following rhyming words. Make a path by drawing a straight line to connect each word from row to row.

1. Draw a line from **START** to the word in row one that rhymes with **snail**.
2. Draw a line to the word in row two that rhymes with **late**.
3. Draw a line to the word in row three that rhymes with **night**.
4. Draw a line to the word in row four that rhymes with **find**.
5. Draw a line to the word in row five that rhymes with **glow**.
6. Draw a line to the word in row six that rhymes with **taste**.
7. Draw a line to the word in row seven that rhymes with **garden**.
8. Draw a line to the word in row eight that rhymes with **would**.
9. Draw a line to the word in row nine that rhymes with **strange**.
10. Draw a line to the word in row ten that rhymes with **took**.
11. Draw a line to the **melon patch**.

START

1.	tall	trail	smile	small	snake
2.	bat	lake	let	lane	bait
3.	fit	ripe	high	kite	neat
4.	mind	friend	fin	mine	line
5.	goat	lone	toe	brown	toad
6.	hat	face	waist	mass	take
7.	button	start	bottom	growing	harden
8.	wool	hood	hide	mud	food
9.	range	sang	rain	string	hang
10.	tooth	poke	hook	coat	lock

FE11004 © 1999 Fearon Teacher Aids

Sneaky Snail Activities

New Nouns

Have students circle all the nouns in the poem. For each noun, have students write one or more synonyms. A *synonym* is a word that means the same, or nearly the same. Encourage students to use a dictionary and/or thesaurus to find synonyms.

What Happened Then?

Have students write or draw what they think happened to the sneaky snail.

Up Close and Personal

Invite someone who has snails bring some in a small aquarium or glass bowl to class for students to observe closely. Have them note their observations, then check reference materials for more information.

All About Snails

Have students use reference materials to find out more about snails. Have them draw one type of snail and write five to ten facts about snails on the page. Have them copy one fact on a 3" x 5" (7.5 cm x 12.5 cm) index card.

Snail Trail

Copy and cut out the snail pattern on the next page. Attach the snail to one corner of a bulletin board. Have students attach their 3" x 5" (7.5 cm x 12.5 cm) index cards with snail facts behind the snail to make a snail trail.

Super Snail to the Rescue!

Have students create a comic strip that takes place in a mysterious garden where Super Snail is the superhero. Have them write short adventure stories in comic-strip format and illustrate the stories.

Related Reading

Life of the Snail by Theres Buholzer (Carolrhoda, 1987).

Snail Saves the Day by John Stadler (Harper, 1985).

Snails by Jens Oleson (Silver, 1986).

Snails and Slugs by Chris Henwood (Watts, 1988).

Related Topics

snails, melons, gardens, mysteries, night, dancing

FE11004 © 1999 Fearon Teacher Aids

Sneaky Snail Pattern

FE11004 © 1999 Fearon Teacher Aids

Soda Pop

Options

A	B	
All	All	Zip! Snap! Fizzle, fizzle, Squirt, splash, slop!
1	1	Who shook my can of soda pop?
All	All	Quick! Quick! Someone fetch a mop.
	2	The soda is squirting Out of the top!
All	All	Zip! Snap! Fizzle, fizzle, Squirt, splash, slop!
2	1	The squirting can Is starting to hop.
	All	Quick! Quick! Someone make it stop!
All	2	Before we're flooded With soda pop!

FE11004 © 1999 Fearon Teacher Aids

Soda Pop Puzzle

Find words from the poem in the puzzle. Move up, down, forward, backward, or diagonally, drawing a line to connect the droplets to form words. Each space is used only once.

◆ **Hint:** The dots show the first letter of each word. Write the words in the soda can as you find them.

FE11004 © 1999 Fearon Teacher Aids

Soda Pop Activities

Five Hundred Flavors

Have students brainstorm different flavors (banana, vanilla, apple, chocolate, caramel, peanut, and so on). Write the list on chart paper. Students can use this list for ideas for the next activity.

Invent a New Flavor

Blueberry-Apple? Fizzle-Flavored Fungus? What new flavor of soda would students like to create? Students can design a label for the soda can on 5" x 9" (12.5 cm x 22.5 cm) construction paper. Remind students to list the ingredients and include a catchy name or logo for the product. Cover a real soda can with the construction-paper label. Tape or glue in place.

Let students present their new flavor soda to the class. Take a poll. How many in the class would be willing to give the new flavor a try?

Buy Me

Provide several full-page color ads for different products. Hold a class discussion about how the ads are designed to appeal to people and sell the product. Point out how color was used; the type of people or setting pictured; and the amount, style, and content of the text.

Students can write magazine ads for an existing flavor of soda or for the ones they invented. Remind them to include the name of the product and the main ingredients. Be sure they tell why people should buy this product.

Soda-Can Collage

Cut a sheet of construction paper in the shape of a large can of soda. Have students look through magazines and grocery ads and cut out colorful pictures of soda and other beverages. Arrange and glue the pictures on the paper to make a collage.

Soda Survey

Have students take a poll of friends and family members to determine their favorite kind of soda. Students can make a bar graph or pie chart to show the results.

Related Topics

soda pop, beverages, containers, food, messes, labels, advertising

FE11004 © 1999 Fearon Teacher Aids

Trash Can Creature

Options		
A	**B**	
1	1	Here's a story we want to tell, So take your time and listen well.
2	2	This tale could be a front page feature, **"The Day Our Trash Can Became a Creature."**
All	All	The trash can started to gurgle and bubble. We all knew there'd soon be trouble.
Leader Girls Boys	Leader Girls Boys	"Step back quickly!" our teacher cried. "Oh my gosh!" the girls all sighed. "Close your eyes," the guys replied. "Our trash can has come alive!"
1	3	In our classroom we never stopped, 'Til that trash can was filled to the top.
2	4	But on that day the can did explode, With our old papers, it had overflowed.
All	All	The trash can started to gurgle and bubble. We all knew there'd soon be trouble.
Leader Girls Boys	Leader Girls Boys	"Step back quickly!" our teacher cried. "Oh my gosh!" the girls all sighed. "Close your eyes," the guys replied. "Our trash can has come alive!"

FE11004 © 1999 Fearon Teacher Aids

Trash Can Creature *(cont'd)*

1	1	The trash can shook. Out came green smoke. We all knew this was not a joke.
Leader	Leader	About that time our teacher said, "Please stay calm. Don't lose your head."
All	All	The trash can started to gurgle and bubble. We all knew there'd soon be trouble.
Leader Girls Boys	Leader Girls Boys	"Step back quickly!" our teacher cried. "Oh my gosh!" the girls all sighed. "Close your eyes," the guys replied. "Our trash can has come alive!"
1	3	She tried her best, our dear teacher did. To cover that trash can with a lid.
2	4	But it turned into a wild creature, And then it swallowed up our dear teacher.
All	All	The trash can started to gurgle and bubble. We all knew there'd soon be trouble.
Leader Girls Boys	Leader Girls Boys	"Step back quickly!" our teacher cried. "Oh my gosh!" the girls all sighed. "Close your eyes," the guys replied. "Our trash can has come alive!"
1	1 & 2	Today that classroom is locked up tight. We all ran out without a fight.
2	3 & 4	Green smoke still seeps out under the door, And we never saw our teacher anymore.

FE11004 © 1999 Fearon Teacher Aids

Reproducible

Trash Can Creature Puzzle

As far as we know, the teacher is still trapped inside the classroom with the trash can creature. Follow the directions to send the teacher a message in Morse Code. Morse Code is a system of dots and dashes representing the letters of the alphabet.

Morse Code

·— a	—··· b	—·—· c	—·· d	· e	··—· f	——· g	···· h	·· i	·——— j
—·— k	·—·· l	—— m	—· n	——— o	·——· p	——·— q	·—· r	··· s	— t
··— u	···— v	·—— w	—··— x	—·—— y	——·· z				

1. Write your message here: _____

    _____

2. Rewrite your message in Morse Code. For example: *Be brave* would be written like this:

    —··· ·   —··· ·—· ·— ···· ·

    Leave a small space between each letter and a larger space between each word.

    _____

    _____

    _____

3. Cut off the section with your message in Morse Code. Trade messages with a partner and decode each other's message.

◆ **Bonus:** Decode this message.

    —·· · · ·—··   ··· ·—··   — ···· ·
    ___ ___ ___ ___   ___ ___   ___ ___ ___

    ——· · ——— ——— —··   ·—· ——— ·· —··
    ___ ___ ___ ___   ___ ___ ___ ___

FE11004 © 1999 Fearon Teacher Aids

Trash Can Creature Activities

Trash Can Creature Moving Picture

Students can create moving pictures that show events from the poem. Have them draw vertical lines every ten inches (25 cm) on a long strip of paper to divide it into equal-sized frames for each scene. Draw pictures in order, starting at the beginning of the story, one scene for each frame. After coloring the pictures, attach each end of the paper to an empty paper-towel roll to form a two-handled scroll. Scroll the paper from one tube to the other to create a moving picture.

"Trash Can Swallows Teacher"

Students can write newspaper articles to report what happened in the classroom. Include the teacher's and students' reactions and what occurred at the end. Have students include answers to the six question words: *Who? What? When? Where? Why?* and *How?* Include a headline for the article.

And Then?

Ask students to write or draw what they predict will happen in the classroom and what will become of the teacher and/or the trash can creature.

3-D Trash Can Creatures

Students can make their own trash can creatures from empty soup or vegetable cans. (Be sure the cans do not have sharp edges.) Cover the can with construction paper, then decorate the creature with crayons or markers. Add scraps of paper, yarn, newspapers, and so on, inside the trash can, spilling out to look like trash. Encourage students to use their imaginations to show how the trash can gurgled and bubbled.

Caution!

Students can design warning signs to place outside the classroom featured in the poem. Include a description of what is behind the door and advice to anyone who might want to go inside.

Related Topics

litter, trash removal, pollution, classrooms, danger, schools, teachers

FE11004 © 1999 Fearon Teacher Aids

Who? What?

Options		
A	**B**	
All	1	Who?
		What?
		Where?
		When?
1	All	Reading these words makes my head spin.
All	2	Who?
		What?
		Where?
		Why?
2	All	I want to give up, but teacher says try.
All	1	Who?
		What?
		When?
		Where?
3	All	Reading these words makes me pull out my hair.
All	2	Why?
		What?
		When?
		Who?
4	All	Now my teacher's head is almost bald too.

FE11004 © 1999 Fearon Teacher Aids

Who? What? Puzzle

Use the words from the word bank to fill in the missing **who, what, when, where,** and **why** words in each sentence.

> ## Word Bank
> bug, shark, mice, fish, cookies, morning, night, swamp, kitchen, sea, no cheese, forgot

1. Three _____ in the _____ ate
    (who/what)   (where)

    two _____ since there was _____ .
         (what)   (why)

2. In the _____ swims a big _____ ,
         (where)   (who/what)

    and every _____ he chases little _____ .
              (when)   (what)

3. On a dark _____ , a lightning _____ was lost
            (when)   (who/what)

    in the _____ because he _____ his flashlight.
          (where)   (why)

Write two sentences, leaving blanks for *who, what, when, where,* and *why* words. Write *who, what, when, where,* or *why* under the blanks. Trade papers with a partner and fill in the blanks on each other's papers.

4. _____

   _____

   _____

5. _____

   _____

   _____

FE11004 © 1999 Fearon Teacher Aids   **Reproducible**

Who? What? Coloring Puzzle

Color the spaces in the design according to the Color Key.

Color Key

Yellow = spaces that contain a word that tells **when**

Red = spaces that contain a word that tells **where**

Blue = spaces that contain a word that tells **who** or **what**

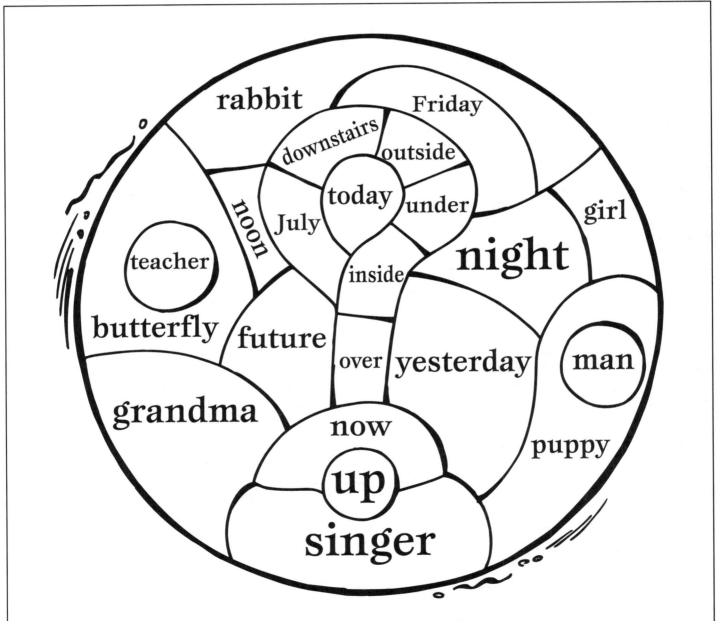

FE11004 © 1999 Fearon Teacher Aids

Who? What? Activities

Who? What? Game

Have students work together in small groups to design and produce a game using *who, what, where, when,* and *why.*

Encourage students to use their imaginations to invent the game. They can use one of the following suggestions or make up a totally different type of game. Remind them to include a list of instructions on how to play the game.

- The game could be on posterboard in game-board format and use dice or a spinner. The words *who, what, where, when,* and *why* could be written on spaces on the game board.

- The game could be a card game like "Go Fish" or a memory game like "Concentration."

- Students could write *who, what, where, when,* and *why* questions on index cards and award points for correct answers.

- The game could involve physical actions or pantomime for the *who, what, when, where,* and *why* words.

Search for the Answers

Have students read short newspaper articles. Have them look for statements that provide answers to *who, what, where, when,* and *why.* On a separate sheet of paper, have students write the word *who,* then answer the question using what they learned from the article. Continue with the words *what, when, where,* and *why,* writing the words and answering the questions.

Acrostic Poems

Invite students to write five acrostic poems using the words *who, what, when, where,* and *why.* Have them write each letter of the words in vertical columns. Title the poems "Who?," "What?," "When?," "Where?," and "Why?" Each letter in the word becomes the first letter in a word or phrase for each line of the poem. The "Who?" poem should use words that describe a person; the "What?" poem should use words that describe an object; and so on.

W	W	W	W	W
H	H	H	H	H
O	A	E	E	Y
	T	N	R	
			E	

Related Topics

questions, information, clues, journalism

FE11004 © 1999 Fearon Teacher Aids

Wiggle, Wiggle, Tooth

Options

A	B	
1	1	I wish I could be Like a goose,
	2	And never have a Tooth get loose.
2	1	I'd never want to Be a moose,
	2	And have a big, back Tooth get loose.
3	1	I'll stop my wishing; It's no use,
	2	And wiggle my small Tooth that's loose.
All	All	Wiggle, wiggle, tooth!

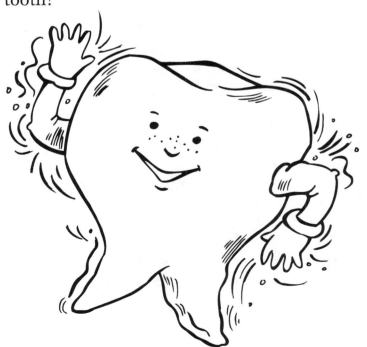

FE11004 © 1999 Fearon Teacher Aids

Wiggle, Wiggle, Tooth Puzzle

Complete the puzzle by using the words from the poem to fill in the missing spaces. Each word is used only once. The words are written from top to bottom, starting with the given letter or ending with the given letter.

For example:

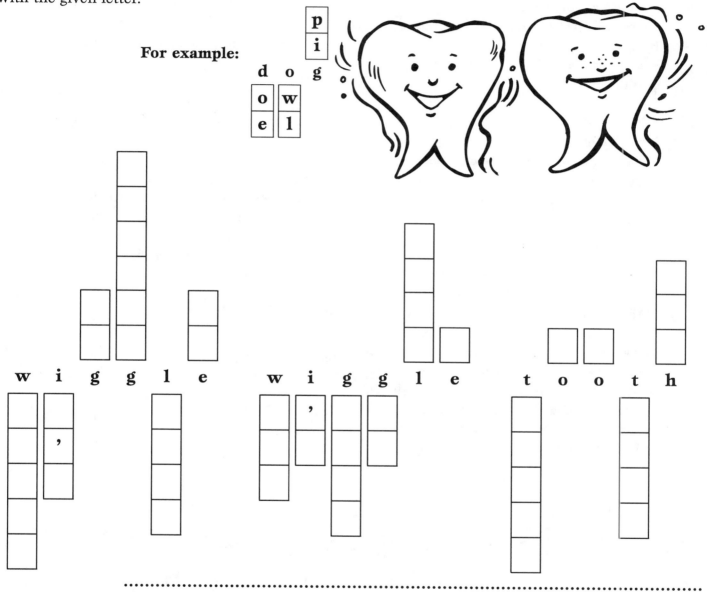

Riddle: What has many teeth but never eats?

Unscramble the letters to find the answer.

m o b c

Answer: A ___ ___ ___ ___

FE11004 © 1999 Fearon Teacher Aids

Wiggle, Wiggle, Tooth Activities

What Would They Say?

Have students draw a picture of a moose and a goose from the poem and add a speech bubble coming from each of their mouths. In each speech bubble students can write what the goose and the moose might say about teeth.

Tooth Specialist

Invite a dentist, dental hygienist, or the school nurse to speak to the class about the importance of taking care of their teeth. Encourage students to participate in the discussion by asking questions.

Parts of a Tooth

Have students use reference materials to find information about teeth and how to take care of them. Have them draw a diagram of a tooth and label its parts, then write a paragraph telling how to correctly take care of teeth and gums. They should include ways to properly clean teeth, types of food that should be eaten or avoided to help keep teeth healthy, and reasons why it is important to visit the dentist regularly.

Loose Tooth Blues

Ask students to write a short descriptive paragraph or poem about the first time they lost a tooth. *What was it like? Was it scary? Was it funny? When and where did it happen?*

Tooth Math

Have students write story problems for the class to solve involving losing and growing teeth. They can write addition, subtraction, multiplication, or division problems. For more challenge, make some of the problems involve two-step operations. Have them write tooth math problems neatly on a piece of paper and exchange papers with a classmate. After solving each other's problems, have students double-check the answers.

Related Reading

Teeth by John Gaskin (Watts, 1984).

Your Teeth by Joan Iveson-Iveson (Watts, 1985).

Related Topics

teeth, dentists, moose, goose

FE11004 © 1999 Fearon Teacher Aids

Woolly Wigglewog

Options
A   B

1	1	Down in the swampy bog, Under a rotten log, Hiding in the misty fog, Snores a woolly wigglewog.
2	2	Wait! Stop! What did you say? A snoring tree frog?
All	All	Nooooo!
1	3	Down in the swampy bog, Under a rotten log, Hiding in the misty fog, Snores a woolly wigglewog.
2	4	Wait! Stop! What did you say? A snoring hound dog?
All	All	Nooooo!

FE11004 © 1999 Fearon Teacher Aids

Woolly Wigglewog *(cont'd)*

1	3	Down in the swampy bog,
		Under a rotten log,
		Hiding in the misty fog,
		Snores a woolly wigglewog.
2	4	Wait! Stop!
		What did you say?
		A snoring groundhog?
All	All	Nooooo!
1	3	Down in the swampy bog,
		Under a rotten log,
		Hiding in the misty fog,
		Snores a woolly wigglewog.
2	4	Wait! Stop!
		What did you say?
		A snoring wigglewog?
All	All	Yeaaaah!
2	All	What's a woolly wigglewog?
1	1	I don't know!

FE11004 © 1999 Fearon Teacher Aids

Woolly Wigglewog Puzzle

Follow the directions to create a picture from the poem. Using watercolors will give the picture a misty, foggy quality.

1. Paint or draw the ground to look like a swampy bog.
2. Paint or draw a rotten log in the center of the bog.
3. Add fog or a large cloud in the sky. Make it look misty.
4. Paint or draw a woolly wigglewog under the log. Use your imagination to draw what you think it may look like. Write *Z*s above its head to show it is snoring.
5. On each of the three signs, draw a picture symbol to show: no tree frog, no hound dog, no groundhog. For example: This sign shows no bike riding.
6. Finish painting or coloring your picture.

FE11004 © 1999 Fearon Teacher Aids

Woolly Wigglewog Activities

Woolly Wigglewog Puppet

Students can use old socks or paper bags to make woolly wigglewog puppets. Provide yarn, buttons, glitter, crepe paper, and scraps of material or construction paper for details. Ask students to share their puppets with the class and have the puppet tell something about what's it like to be a woolly wigglewog.

What's a Woolly Wigglewog?

Ask students to write a description of a woolly wigglewogs. Have them use their imaginations to tell what a woolly wigglewog eats, where it lives, and what it does when it isn't snoring. *How big is a woolly wigglewog? Does it have a tail? fur? Does it climb trees? What sounds does it make when it's awake?*

Tune in for the News

Ask students to imagine they are television reporters. The first woolly wigglewog has just been discovered. As reporters, they must gather the facts and prepare a television news report. Have them prepare a list of questions to ask when they interview the person who discovered the first woolly wigglewog. Remind them to use *who, what, when, where, why,* and *how* questions.

Once the questions are ready, they need to find answers by interviewing the person who discovered the woolly wigglewog. Have them imagine being that person and providing answers to the questions.

And It Rhymes with *Wigglewog*

Ask students to list words and word phrases from the poem that rhyme with *wigglewog*. Have them add other rhyming words or word phrases not found in the poem. Encourage them to make up rhyming words or phrases for other imaginary creatures that might live in the swamp with the woolly wigglewog.

Pet Woolly Wigglewogs

Ask students to imagine they are the owner of a pet store selling woolly wigglewogs. Use words and illustrations to design a newspaper or magazine ad telling people why woolly wigglewogs would make good pets and why everyone should have one. Be sure to list the price and show a picture of a woolly wigglewog.

Related Topics

swamps, animals, discoveries, habitats, mysteries, questions

FE11004 © 1999 Fearon Teacher Aids

Yikes!

Options		
A	**B**	
1	1	I forgot to empty my pockets.
		Mom warned me about this before.
2		I stashed my ball card in my pocket,
		Before I ran out the door.
All	All	Swish! Swash! Slosh!
		My ball card went through the wash.
		Then it went in the dryer,
		And now my ball card is lost!
		Yikes!
1	2	I forgot to empty my pockets.
		Mom warned me about this before.
2		I stashed my homework in my pocket,
		Before I ran out the door.
All	All	Swish! Swash! Slosh!
		My homework went through the wash.
		Then it went in the dryer,
		And now my homework is lost!
		Yikes!
1	3	I forgot to empty my pockets.
		Mom warned me about this before.
2		I stashed my report card in my pocket,
		Before I ran out the door.
All	All	Swish! Swash! Slosh!
		My report card went through the wash.
		Then it went in the dryer,
		And now my report card is lost!
		Yikes!

FE11004 © 1999 Fearon Teacher Aids

Yikes! Puzzle

Search for 21 words from the poem. The words are written up, down, forward, backward, and diagonally. Circle the words as you find them.

```
o  d  r  a  c  l  l  a  b
u  e  m  p  h  t  y  y  d
t  b  e  f  o  r  e  o  e
u  r  p  o  m  h  c  k  n
p  o  c  k  e  t  s  e  r
t  h  s  i  w  s  b  a  a
t  s  o  l  o  t  n  e  w
r  t  o  g  r  o  f  e  f
e  a  o  r  k  e  r  a  n
p  s  w  y  i  k  e  s  d
o  h  e  m  p  t  y  a  o
r  e  s  h  o  i  r  n  o
t  d  w  o  n  m  d  g  r
```

Word Bank
ball
before
card
door
dryer
empty
forgot
homework
lost
mom
now
out
pockets
ran
report
stashed
swish
warned
wash
went
yikes

◆ **Bonus:** Write the unused letters in order from left to right to read a message.

_ _ _ _ _   _ _ _ _ _ _

_ _ _ _ _ _ _ _ _ _ .

FE11004 © 1999 Fearon Teacher Aids

Yikes! Activities

Where Do They Go?

Ask students to imagine that the dryer could talk. Have them write a short interview asking the dryer why it takes things and what it does with the items that disappear, like the baseball card, the homework, and the report card. Have them include the dryer's replies.

The Animated Dryer

Have students draw a picture of the dryer as though it were alive. Give it a face and include a speech bubble coming from the dryer's "mouth." In the bubble, write a comment from the dryer about the disappearance of the items in the poem.

Did It Ever Happen to You?

Ask students to write about something they or a family member mysteriously lost and never found. Have them describe the circumstances of the loss and what they thought might have happened to the item.

The Most Important Appliance

Have students select any one appliance commonly found in people's homes that they think is the most useful. Ask them to give five reasons why they think it is the most useful appliance.

Get Other Opinions

Ask students to predict which appliance other people would consider the most useful. Have them write down their predictions, then take a survey of 10 to 20 friends and family members to find out which appliance other people consider the most useful. Have students make a bar graph or pictograph to display their results. Did their predictions agree with the survey results?

Comparison Shopping

Have students use ads to compare features of various brands and models of one type of appliance. Have them write a summary of their findings to explain which they think is the best buy.

Related Topics

washers, dryers, appliances, lost objects, homework, report cards, baseball cards, pockets

FE11004 © 1999 Fearon Teacher Aids

You and Me*

Options		
A	**B**	
1	1	I see red, You see blue.
	2	I find one, You find two.
	1	Is it me, Or is it you?
2	All	Here I come. Away you run. You help me look for fun. You make me jump and play, In a big and little way.
1	2	You see yellow. I see blue.
	1	You find three. I find two.
	2	You help me. I help you.
2	All	Here I come. Away you run. You help me look for fun. You make me jump and play, In a big and little way.

(*This poem is comprised only of words from the pre-primer Dolch Basic Word List.)

FE11004 © 1999 Fearon Teacher Aids

You and Me Puzzle

Solve the puzzle by writing antonyms from the Word Bank for each clue. *Antonyms* are words that mean the opposite, like *sleep* and *wake*.

> ## Word Bank
> right, thin, down, good, over, happy, hot, night, lost,
> tall, no, young, dark, go, top, big, off, soft, out, front

Across

1. up
5. under
7. found
8. bad
10. fat
13. stop
14. day
16. bottom
19. back

Down

2. in
3. yes
4. old
6. left
9. light
11. sad
12. little
15. cold
17. on
18. hard
20. short

You and Me Activities

You and Me Adventure

Ask students to write about an adventure they had with a friend. Tell what happened and why it was exciting. Illustrate the story.

Friend Wanted

Good Friend Wanted: Must be loyal and truthful, and like dogs, pizza, hopscotch, and hiking. I can help with math homework and like to share my button collection. I also make the best pizza in the world.

Write the above ad on the board. Have students write their own ads that include information about what traits they think a good friend should have and what benefits that person would receive if he or she became their friend.

Even When . . .

Ask students to brainstorm an ending to this sentence: *Friends like you even when . . . (. . . you forgot their birthday, . . . you are having a bad hair day).* Write their responses on chart paper.

Friends Should . . .

Ask students to list characteristics they feel are important for friends to have. Have them circle the one characteristic they feel is most important and explain why.

Venn Diagram

Have students complete the Venn diagram on the next page. In the part of the circle marked *you*, have students list the traits, opinions, and ideas of a friend that they do not share *(likes red best, plays the piano . . .).*

In the part of the circle marked *me*, have them write the traits, opinions, and ideas that they have, but their friend doesn't share *(favorite color is green, likes to read . . .).*

In the part where the circles intersect *(us)*, have them write things they and their friend have in common *(like rap music, like pizza, don't like anchovies . . .).*

Related Topics

friends, opposites, favorite things, adventures

FE11004 © 1999 Fearon Teacher Aids

You and Me Venn Diagram

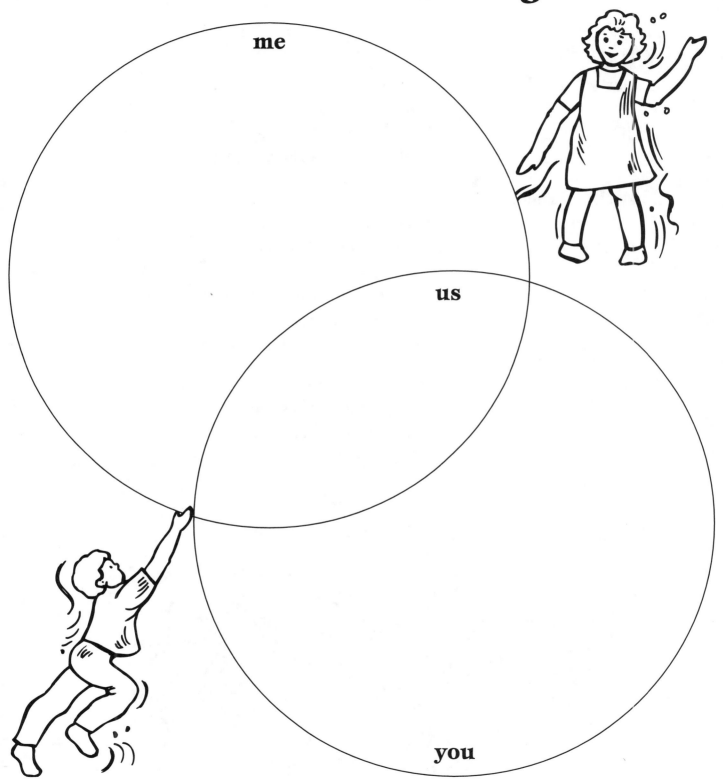

me

us

you

FE11004 © 1999 Fearon Teacher Aids

Ziggle Wiggle

Options

A	B	
Leader	Leader	Are you ready, are you set?
		On your mark, don't forget!
All	All	Chuckle, chuckle, giggle, giggle,
		Let's all do the ziggle wiggle!
Leader	Leader	Ready, stand . . .
	1	Count down, 10, 9, 8,
		Do not start! You must wait!
	2	7, 6, 5, 4,
		I can't stand still anymore.
	3	3, 2, and number 1,
		Now we're ready for some fun.
Leader	Leader	Ready, Set, Go!
All		Wiggle, jiggle, twist, and giggle,
		Turn around, reach up and down.
		Wiggle, giggle, jump, and jiggle.
Leader	Leader	Keep on ziggling . . .
All		1, 2, 3, 4, 5, 6,
		7, 8, 9, and 10.
		Let's sit down and start again.

Ziggle Wiggle *(cont'd)*

Leader	Leader	Are you ready, are you set?
		On your mark, don't forget!
All	All	Chuckle, chuckle, giggle, giggle,
		Let's all do the ziggle wiggle!
Leader	Leader	Ready, stand . . .
All	1	Count down, 10, 9, 8,
		Do not start! You must wait!
	2	7, 6, 5, 4,
		I can't stand still anymore.
	3	3, 2, and number 1,
		Now we're ready for some fun.
Leader	Leader	Ready, Set, Go!
All		Wiggle, jiggle, twist, and giggle,
		Turn around, reach up and down.
		Wiggle, giggle, jump, and jiggle.
Leader	Leader	Keep on ziggling . . .
All		1, 2, 3, 4, 5, 6,
		7, 8, 9, and 10.
		Let's sit down. It's time to end!

FE11004 © 1999 Fearon Teacher Aids

Reproducible

Ziggle Wiggle Puzzle

Find the points on the graph to spell action words from the poem. For each number pair, the first number is on the horizontal axis or line, and the second number is on the vertical axis. The point where the two lines intersect has a letter. On the next page, write the letter for each number pair to spell out an action word.

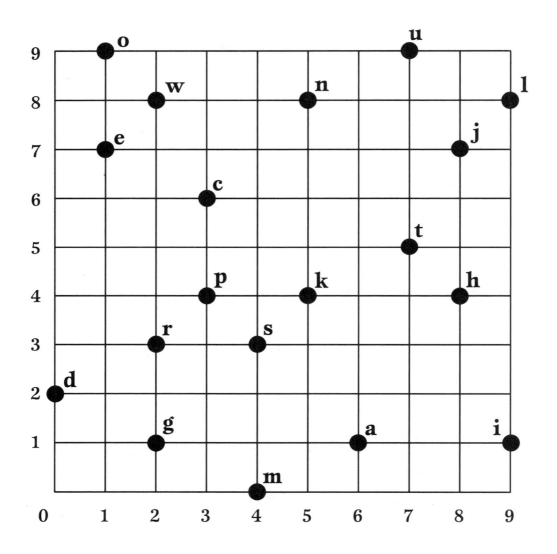

Reproducible   FE11004 © 1999 Fearon Teacher Aids

Ziggle Wiggle Puzzle *(cont'd)*

1. $\overline{}$ $\overline{}$ $\overline{}$ $\overline{}$ $\overline{}$
   (7,5) (2,8) (9,1) (4,3) (7,5)

2. $\overline{}$ $\overline{}$ $\overline{}$ $\overline{}$
   (8,7) (7,9) (4,0) (3,4)

3. $\overline{}$ $\overline{}$ $\overline{}$ $\overline{}$ $\overline{}$ $\overline{}$ $\overline{}$
   (3,6) (8,4) (7,9) (3,6) (5,4) (9,8) (1,7)

4. $\overline{}$ $\overline{}$ $\overline{}$
   (4,3) (9,1) (7,5)

5. $\overline{}$ $\overline{}$ $\overline{}$ $\overline{}$ $\overline{}$ $\overline{}$
   (8,7) (9,1) (2,1) (2,1) (9,8) (1,7)

6. $\overline{}$ $\overline{}$ $\overline{}$ $\overline{}$ $\overline{}$
   (4,3) (7,5) (6,1) (5,8) (0,2)

7. $\overline{}$ $\overline{}$ $\overline{}$ $\overline{}$ $\overline{}$
   (2,3) (1,7) (6,1) (3,6) (8,4)

8. $\overline{}$ $\overline{}$ $\overline{}$ $\overline{}$ $\overline{}$
   (3,6) (1,9) (7,9) (5,8) (7,5)

9. $\overline{}$ $\overline{}$ $\overline{}$ $\overline{}$
   (7,5) (7,9) (2,3) (5,8)

10. $\overline{}$ $\overline{}$ $\overline{}$ $\overline{}$ $\overline{}$ $\overline{}$
    (2,8) (9,1) (2,1) (2,1) (9,8) (1,7)

Ziggle Wiggle Activities

How to Ziggle Wiggle

Make copies of the "Ziggle Wiggle" poem for each student. After reading and participating in the Ziggle Wiggle chant, have students write actions on the right side of the page describing how to do the Ziggle Wiggle. They can describe the actions they actually did or ones they think would work as well or better.

Ziggle Wiggle Dance Steps

Have students work together in small groups to choose Ziggle Wiggle music and make up dance steps to go with the music. Have groups demonstrate the Ziggle Wiggle to the class.

Ziggle Wiggle Break

Ask students to write a persuasive paragraph to explain why it would be a good idea for teachers to give students a Ziggle Wiggle break every day. If students are persuasive enough, they might really get a few Ziggle Wiggle breaks.

Ziggle Wiggle Contest

Have students design posters to advertise a Ziggle Wiggle Contest. They should describe the contest and prizes, and give the date, time, and location.

Ziggle Wiggle Clothes

The new Ziggle Wiggle dance is the latest fad. Now everyone wants to buy Ziggle Wiggle clothes. What do they look like? That's for students to decide when they draw the latest Ziggle Wiggle fashions for boys and girls.

Ziggle Wiggle Spokesperson

The Ziggle Wiggle craze needs a spokesperson. Who should it be? A famous movie star? An athlete? A person from history, like Napoleon? Have students find or draw a picture of who they think should be the Ziggle Wiggle spokesperson. Add a speech bubble. Write words the spokesperson would say about the Ziggle Wiggle.

What's the Next Verse?

Grandmothers do it, babies do too.
If they can ziggle wiggle, so can you.

Write the above couplet on chart paper. Have each student write a verse using the same rhythm and rhyme. When they have their couplets "polished," ask them to add the couplets to the poem on the chart paper.

Related Topics

dancing, counting, movements, following directions, numbers

Zippo

Options

A	B	
1	1	A hippo named Zippo Lives down at the zoo.
2		And Zippo, the hippo Only eats food that is blue.
1	2	Oh Zippo, the hippo Loves jelly that's blue,
2		Blue cheese and blueberries, Blue cornflowers too.
1	3	The zookeeper searches For food that will do.
2		'Cause Zippo, the hippo Wants new food to chew.
1	4	Zippo eats plenty, Tho' choices are few.
2		Eating tons of blue foods Have turned his skin blue.
1	All	No, I'm not joking, This really is true.
2		The skin of this hippo Has turned a bright blue.
1	All	If you were the zookeeper, What would you do?
2		Why does Zippo eat blue food? I haven't a clue.

Zippo Puzzle

Zippo not only loves to eat blue food, but he also likes other blue items too. Listed below are the meanings for words that have the word *blue* in them. Match each meaning with a word on the right by writing the letter for the word in the blank. Feel free to use the dictionary if you need it.

_____ 1. pirate   n. blue bonnet

_____ 2. small fruit   u. blue blood

_____ 3. royalty   c. bluecoat

_____ 4. fish   b. Bluebeard

_____ 5. policeman   o. bluebill

_____ 6. duck   e. bluegill

_____ 7. flower   l. blueberry

_____ 8. flat cap   r. bluebell

_____

_____ 9. bird   o. blue racer

_____ 10. plan or drawing   e. bluebird

_____ 11. snake   f. blue jay

_____ 12. first place   r. blue flag

_____ 13. songbird   s. bluegrass

_____ 14. iris flower   w. blue ribbon

_____ 15. region or music   l. blueprint

◆ **Bonus:** Read down the letters of the answers. If the answers are correct, they will spell Zippo's favorite blossom.

Answer: _____

         FE11004 © 1999 Fearon Teacher Aids

Zippo Activities

Food for Zippo

What will Zippo eat this week? Remember, he only eats foods that are blue. Have students make a daily menu for one week listing the foods and amounts of each that the zookeeper will provide for Zippo. Since a full-grown hippo can weigh more than 8,000 pounds, it needs 300 to 400 pounds of food a day. Be sure he gets enough!

Blue Day

Celebrate "Blue Day." Invite students to make decorations from blue crepe paper and construction paper. Students can wear blue clothing and bring blue snacks to share with the class.

Serve blue milk and cookies: Make blue frosting by adding a few drops of blue food coloring to white frosting. Frost animal crackers and add blue sprinkles. Turn milk blue by adding a few drops of blue food coloring to a pint of milk. The milk will taste the same, but it will certainly look strange.

What Will Happen Next?

Ask students to predict what might happen next to Zippo. Will Zippo always remain blue? Will he change his eating habits? Will he have an adventure in the wild blue yonder? Students can write or draw their predictions and share them with the class.

What If?

Students can answer this "what if" question or write and answer one of their own. *What if Zippo, the hippo, went to the town where all the cows wear orange tennis shoes?*

Welcome to the Zoo

The zookeeper would like more people to visit Zippo, the hippo and the other animals at the zoo. Ask students to design a poster promoting the zoo. Have them create a name and logo for the zoo, write a jingle to get people to come, and tell about Zippo and any other unusual animals that might also be in the zoo.

More About Hippos

The word *hippopotamus* means "river horse." Have students use reference materials to find other facts about hippopotamuses. Have them trace and cut out the hippo pattern on the next page and write several facts they learned on the hippo. Be sure they color it blue when they're through. Use the blue hippos for a bulletin-board display.

Related Reading

Harvey the Hiccupping Hippopotamus by Tanya Baker and Carlton Holm (Barron's, 1992).

Hippo by C. H. Trevisick (Raintree, 1980).

Hippo by Marianne Johnston (PowerKids, 1997).

Hippopotamus by Sally Banks (Grolier, 1990).

Related Topics

hippopotamus, zoo, animals, food, blue, colors

FE11004 © 1999 Fearon Teacher Aids

Hippo Pattern

FE11004 © 1999 Fearon Teacher Aids

Mister Zoat, the Stoat

Options

A	B	
1	1	Mister Zoat, the stoat, Is a weasel who floats.
2		He floats in the moat,
	All	'Cause he has no boat.
1	2	Mister Zoat, the stoat, Likes to eat rolled oats.
2		He eats as he floats,
	All	'Cause he has no boat.
1	3	Mister Zoat, the stoat's Rolled oats got soaked.
2		They bloated as they floated,
	All	'Cause he had no boat.
1	1	Mister Zoat, the stoat, Ate bloated rolled oats.
2		They got stuck in his throat,
	All	'Cause he had no boat.
1	2	Along came a goat, With a root-beer float.
2		He couldn't help Zoat,
	All	'Cause he had no boat.
1	3	Mister Zoat, the stoat, Floated over to the goat.
2		Zoat drank the float,
	All	Then he thanked that goat.
1	1	This tale of the stoat,
	2	Ends on a glad note.
2	3	'Cause that root-beer float Cleared up Zoat's throat.
	All	(But he still has no boat!)

FE11004 © 1999 Fearon Teacher Aids

Mister Zoat, the Stoat Puzzle

Many words contain smaller words. In the poem there are many words that contain the smaller word *oat*. Fill in each root-beer float glass below to see how many words you can build by adding one or more letters at the beginning of the small word. Check your dictionary for the correct spelling.

1. *oat* Zoat

2. *ate* date

3. *ear* bear

4. *eat* beat

5. *are* bare

Give yourself a point for each correct word you wrote. What is your total score?

    30 or less: Try to find more.
    31–33:   Good work!
    34–36:   Super!
    37 or more: Fantastic!

FE11004 © 1999 Fearon Teacher Aids

Mister Zoat, the Stoat Activities

More About Stoats

Have students use reference materials to learn more about stoats or other types of weasels (mink, ermine, ferrets). *Where do they live? What do they eat? How large are they? How do they use camouflage?* Students can write short reports and add illustrations.

Do Oats Float? Do Oats Bloat?

What happens when oats get wet? Do they float? Do they bloat? Students can find out by adding ¼ cup (63 mL) of rolled oats to one cup (250 mL) of room-temperature water in a plastic bowl. Have students predict what will happen before they try the experiment, then report what happened after they finish the experiment. Have them try changing the water temperature. *Do oats bloat more or less in hot water than in cold water? Do oats float better in hot water than in cold?*

Mrs. Babbitt, the Rabbit

Students can write their own rhyming poems similar to "Mister Zoat, the Stoat." Have them decide on an animal and a rhyming name, like *Ms. Laire, the Hare* or *Mister Zink, the Skink*. Once they have a character, have them make a list of rhyming words to use as they write their poems.

Tell Me Why

Ask students to write an imaginary story to explain why animals like stoats and snowshoe rabbits change from brown to white in the winter.

Write Another Verse

Using words ending in *-oat* students wrote on the Mister Zoat, the Stoat Puzzle, have them write one more verse for "Mister Zoat, the Stoat." The new verse could go anywhere in the poem before the last line.

Did He Ever Get a Boat?

Did Mister Zoat ever get a boat? How did he get it? If he didn't get one, why not? Have students write or draw an answer.

Related Reading

The Lion and the Stoat by Paul O. Zelinsky (Greenwillow, 1984).

Related Topics

camouflage, chameleons, stoats, weasels, boats, root beer, goats

FE11004 © 1999 Fearon Teacher Aids

Answer Key

Cupcake Critter Puzzle, page 3

The only word with the long *i* sound in the poem is *wild*.

1. litter, sitter
2. in, it
3. lid, bit
4. wild, live
5. critter, quitter, or glitter
6. glitter, shiver

Bonus riddle: A litter knitter

Cupcake Critter Words, page 4

ace	air	ape	are	art
ate	cake	cap	cape	car
care	cart	cat	crack	cracker
crate	creek	crick	cup	cur
cure	cut	cute	cuter	cutter
ear	eat	ice	ire	kit
kite	pace	pacer	pack	packer
pair	pare	part	pat	pate
patter	pea	peace	peak	pear
peat	peck	peek	peer	pet
pick	pie	pier	pit	pitter
puck	pure	put	putter	race
racer	rack	rake	raker	rap
rat	rate	reap	rear	rice
rip	ripe	rut	tack	take
taker	tap	tape	tart	tarter
tat	teak	tear	tick	ticker
tie	tip	tire	trace	track
trap	treat	tree	trick	trip
tripe	trite	truce	truck	true
tuck				

Hey Spooky Spider! Puzzle, page 7

across	down	up	backward
2. fright	1. worried	10. spider	11. chair
7. crawling	3. tonight	13. find	
8. mess	4. harm		
12. spooky	5. me		
	6. arm		
	7. close		
	9. sleep		

Let's Sneak a Peek Puzzle, page 10

Present: a secret spy kit

Manatee Magic Puzzle, page 14

1. starfish
2. catfish
3. angelfish
4. jellyfish
5. toadfish
6. swordfish
7. sunfish
8. dogfish
9. shellfish
10. goldfish
11. batfish
12. sawfish
13. sailfish
14. moonfish
15.–18. Answers will vary.

Mixed-Up Martian Puzzle, page 18

(order will vary)

1. Mars, jars, stars
2. made, parade
3. meal, real
4. street, meet, meat, treat, eat
5. head, instead
6. confetti, spaghetti
7. three, he

Message: Eat meat; it's a treat!

Moody Moon Puzzles, pages 21 and 22

Riddle #1

A. sun
B. fade
C. moon
D. new
E. gibbous
F. quarter

Answer: moonsters

Riddle #2

G. laugh
H. looks
I. half
J. full

Answer: U.S.A. flag

FE11004 © 1999 Fearon Teacher Aids

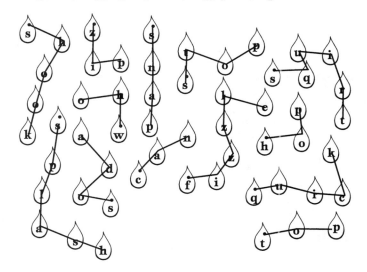

Riddle #3

K. moody   O. smile
L. silly   P. today
M. please   Q. phase
N. change
Answer: moon pie

Mud Pie, Moon Pie Puzzle, page 27

A. blueberry, chocolate, eclair, pumpkin: coconut
B. best, county, first, lightest, their: cherry
C. apple, banana, first, Granny, surprise, won: strawberry
D. peach, pear, pie, prize, pumpkin: pecan

Oh Brother! Puzzle, page 32

1. judge
2. little
3. brother
4. holding/he
5. grudge
6. call/chocolate
7. hurry
8. fudge
9. play
10. oh
11. wall
12. ate
13. smudge
14. stubborn
15. hands
16. blamed
17. messy
18. bribe

Orange Tennis Shoes Puzzle, page 35

1. grape
2. lemon
3. carrot
4. tomato
5. pear
6. apple
7. prune
8. grapefruit
9. strawberry
10. pineapple

Pop! Puzzle, page 38

1. chewed
2. balloons
3. could
4. bought
5. bubbles
6. wanted
7. blew
8. stop
9. went

Rappin' Rabbit Puzzle, page 41

1. Blue Hat Rap
2. No Trap Rap
3. Red Rap Race
4. Rappin' Hop Hop
5. Carrot Chomp Rap
6. Wild Rabbit Rap
7. Happy Hare Hop Rap
8. Real Cool Bunny Rap

Cuckoo Time Puzzle, page 44

1. eyes, them, this, time
2. does, head, like, open
3. shake, shut, slap, stand
4. clock, close, clown, crazy
5. knee, nut, sit, when, who
6. cuckoo, down, please, shut
Answer: Time to buy a new clock!

Saguaro Cactus Puzzle, page 50

1. hot
2. cactus
3. dry
4. saguaro
5. pear
6. desert
7. ouch
8. Sonoran
9. sharp
10. prickly
11. spines
12. friend

Snapdragon Fly Puzzle, page 54

1. fly
2. dragon
3. sun
4. teach
5. wing
6. ground
7. snap
8. pulled
9. down
10. silly
11. home
12. touch
13. tall
14. broken
15. grow
Answer: a snapping turtle

Sneaky Snail Puzzle, page 58

1. trail
2. bait
3. kite
4. mind
5. toe
6. waist
7. harden
8. hood
9. range
10. hook

Soda Pop Puzzle, page 62

Word order will vary: shook, zip, splash, who, soda, snap, can, stop, squirt, fizzle, hop, quick, top

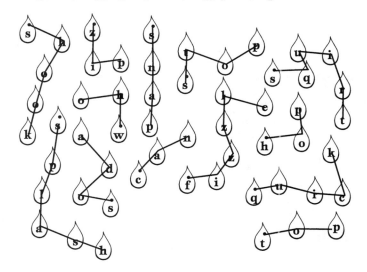

Trash Can Creature Puzzle, page 66

Message: Keep up the good work.

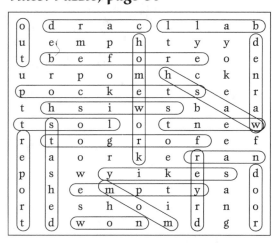

Who? What? Puzzle, page 69

Answers may vary.

1. mice, kitchen, cookies, no cheese
2. sea, shark, morning/night, fish
3. night, bug, swamp, forgot

Who? What? Coloring Puzzle, page 70

Yellow—Friday, today, July, noon, night, future, yesterday, now

Red—downstairs, outside, under, inside, over, up

Blue—teacher, butterfly, rabbit, girl, man, puppy, singer, grandma

The picture should contain a red question mark.

Wiggle, Wiggle, Tooth Puzzle, page 73

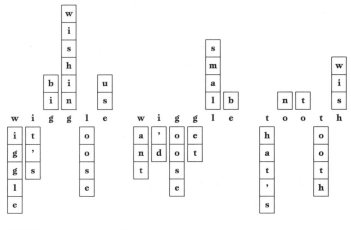

Riddle Answer: comb

Woolly Wigglewog Puzzle, page 77

Answers will vary.

Yikes! Puzzle, page 80

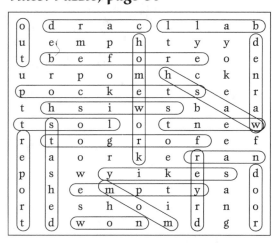

Message: Empty your pocket before washing.

You and Me Puzzle, page 83

across	down	
1. down	2. out	15. hot
4. over	3. no	17. off
7. lost	4. young	18. soft
8. good	6. right	20. tall
10. thin	9. dark	
13. go	11. happy	
14. front	12. big	
16. top		
19. front		

Ziggle Wiggle Puzzle, page 88

1. twist	6. stand
2. jump	7. reach
3. chuckle	8. count
4. sit	9. turn
5. jiggle	10. wiggle

Zippo Puzzle, page 92

1. b	9. f
2. l	10. l
3. u	11. o
4. e	12. w
5. c	13. e
6. o	14. r
7. r	15. s
8. n	

Answer: blue cornflowers

Mister Zoat, the Stoat Puzzle, page 96

(possible answers)

1. bloat, boat, coat, float, gloat, goat, houseboat, moat, rowboat, stoat, throat, topcoat
2. cognate, create, estate, fate, hate, inflate, Kate, late, mate, narrate, pate, plate, pirate, primate, rate, relate, situate, slate, state, sulfate
3. appear, blear, clear, dear, disappear, fear, gear, hear, near, nuclear, pear, rear, smear, spear, tear, underwear, wear, year
4. bleat, cheat, cleat, defeat, feat, great, heat, meat, neat, seat, treat, wheat
5. aware, beware, blare, care, dare, Delaware, fanfare, fare, flare, glare, hardware, hare, mare, Medicare, pare, prepare, scare, share, software, stare, unaware, ware, welfare

FE11004 © 1999 Fearon Teacher Aids